BIG DATA, BIG ANALYTICS

WILEY CIO SERIES

Founded in 1807, John Wiley & Sons is the oldest independent publishing company in the United States. With offices in North America, Europe, Asia, and Australia, Wiley is globally committed to developing and marketing print and electronic products and services for our customers' professional and personal knowledge and understanding.

The Wiley CIO series provides information, tools, and insights to IT executives and managers. The products in this series cover a wide range of topics that supply strategic and implementation guidance on the latest technology trends, leadership, and emerging best practices.

Titles in the Wiley CIO series include:

The Agile Architecture Revolution: How Cloud Computing, REST-Based SOA, and Mobile Computing Are Changing Enterprise IT by Jason Bloomberg

Big Data, Big Analytics: Emerging Business Intelligence and Analytic Trends for Today's Businesses by Michele Chambers, Ambiga Dhiraj, and Michael Minelli

The Chief Information Officer's Body of Knowledge: People, Process, and Technology by Dean Lane

CIO Best Practices: Enabling Strategic Value with Information Technology by Joe Stenzel, Randy Betancourt, Gary Cokins, Alyssa Farrell, Bill Flemming, Michael H. Hugos, Jonathan Hujsak, and Karl D. Schubert

The CIO Playbook: Strategies and Best Practices for IT Leaders to Deliver Value by Nicholas R. Colisto

Enterprise IT Strategy, + Website: An Executive Guide for Generating Optimal ROI from Critical IT Investments by Gregory J. Fell

Executive's Guide to Virtual Worlds: How Avatars Are Transforming Your Business and Your Brand by Lonnie Benson

Innovating for Growth and Value: How CIOs Lead Continuous Transformation in the Modern Enterprise by Hunter Muller

IT Leadership Manual: Roadmap to Becoming a Trusted Business Partner by Alan R. Guibord

Managing Electronic Records: Methods, Best Practices, and Technologies by Robert F. Smallwood

BIG DATA, BIG ANALYTICS

EMERGING BUSINESS INTELLIGENCE AND
ANALYTIC TRENDS FOR TODAY'S BUSINESSES

Michael Minelli

Michele Chambers

Ambiga Dhiraj

WILEY

John Wiley & Sons, Inc.

Published by John Wiley & Sons, Inc., Hoboken, New Jersey.
Published simultaneously in Canada.

For general information on our other products and services or for technical support, please contact our Customer Care Department within the United States at (800) 762-2974, outside the United States at (317) 572-3993 or fax (317) 572-4002.

Wiley publishes in a variety of print and electronic formats and by print-on-demand. Some material included with standard print versions of this book may not be included in e-books or in print-on-demand. If this book refers to media such as a CD or DVD that is not included in the version you purchased, you may download this material at http://booksupport.wiley.com. For more information about Wiley products, visit www.wiley.com.

Library of Congress Cataloging-in-Publication Data

Minelli, Michael, 1974-
    Big data, big analytics : emerging business intelligence and analytic trends for today's businesses / Michael Minelli, Michele Chambers, Ambiga Dhiraj.
        pages   cm
    Includes bibliographical references and index.
    ISBN 978-1-118-14760-3 (cloth); ISBN 978-1-118-22583-7 (ebk);
ISBN 978-1-118-23915-5 (ebk); ISBN 978-1-118-26381-5 (ebk)
        1. Business intelligence.   2. Information technology.   3. Data processing.
4. Data mining.   5. Strategic planning.   I. Chambers, Michele.   II. Dhiraj, Ambiga, 1975-III. Title.
    HD38.7.M565   2013
    658.4'72—dc23

                                                                    2012044882

Printed in the United States of America

10 9 8 7 6 5 4 3

To my wife Jenny and our three incredible children, Jack, Madeline, and Max. Also to my parents, who have always been there for me.

—Mike

To my son Cole, who is the light of my life and the person who taught me empathy. Also to my adopted family and support system, Lisa Patrick, Pei Yee Cheng, and Patrick Thean. Finally, to my colleagues Bill Zannine, Brian Hess, Jon Niess, Matt Rollender, Kevin Kostuik, Krishnan Parasuraman, Mario Inchiosa, Thomas Baeck, Thomas Dinsmore, and Usama Fayyad, for their generous support.

—Michele

To Mu Sigmans all around the world for their passion toward building the decision sciences industry.

—Ambiga

CONTENTS

FOREWORD: BIG DATA AND CORPORATE EVOLUTION

When my friend Mike Minelli asked me to write this foreword I wasn't sure at first what I should put on paper. Forewords are often one part book summary and one part overview of the field. But when I read the draft Mike sent me I realized that this is a really good book, and it doesn't need either of those. Without any additional help from me it will give you plenty of insight into what is happening and why it's happening now, and it will help you see the possibilities for your industry in this transition to a data-centric age. Also, the book is just full of practical suggestions for what you can do about them. But perhaps there's an opportunity to establish a wider context. To explore what Big Data means across a broad arc of technological advancement. So rather than bore you with a summary of a book you're going to read anyway, I'll try to daub a bit of paint onto the big picture of what it all might mean.

This foreword is based on the thesis that Big Data isn't merely another technology. It isn't just another gift box en route to the world's systems integrators via the conveyor belt of Gartner hype cycles. I believe Big Data will follow digital computing and internetworking to take its place as the third epoch of the information age, and in doing so it will fundamentally alter the trajectory of corporate evolution. The corporation is about to undergo a change analogous to the rise of consciousness in humans.

So let's start at the beginning. The Industrial Age was an era of vast changes in society. We harnessed first steam and then electricity as prime movers to unleash astonishing increases in productivity. The result was the first sustained growth of wealth in human history.

Those early industrial concerns required vast pools of labor that gradually grew more specialized. To coordinate the efforts of all of those people, management developed systems of rules and hierarchy of authority. At massive scale the corporation was no longer the direct exercise of an owner's will, it was a kind of organism.

It was an organism whose systems of control were born out of the Napoleonic bureaucracy of the French State and its emphasis on specialized function, fixed rules, and rigid hierarchy. The "bureau" in bureaucracy literally means desk, and paper was both the storage mechanism in them and the signaling mechanism between them.

The bureaucracy was a form of organization that could process stimuli at scale and coordinate masses of participants, but it was, and remains today, severely limited in its evolutionary progress. Bureaucracy is the nematode of human industrial organization.

With over 24,000 species the nematode is a plentiful and adaptable round worm whose nervous system typically consists of 302 neurons. A mere 20 of those neurons are in its pharyngeal nervous system, the part that serves as a rudimentary brain. Yet it is able to maintain homeostasis, direct movement, detect information in its environment, create complex responses, and even manage some basic learning. So, it's a nice approximation for the bureaucratic corporation.

Despite its display of complex behaviors the nematode is of course completely unaware of them in any conscious sense. Its actions, like those of a bureaucracy, are reactive and dispositional. A worm bumps into something and is stimulated. Neurons fire. Worm reacts. It moves away or maybe eats what it bumped. Likewise shelves go empty and an order is placed. Papers move between desks. Trucks arrive. Shelves get replenished.

Worms and corporations are both complex event-processing engines, but they are largely deterministic. The corporation is evolving though, becoming more aware of its surroundings and emergent in its reactions. The information age, or the second industrial age, has been a major part of that.

In 1954 Joe Glickauf of Arthur Andersen implemented a payroll system for the General Electric Corporation on a UNIVAC 1 digital electronic computer. He thus introduced the computational epoch of the information age to the American corporation. (Incidentally, also creating the IT consulting industry.) Throughout the 1950s other corporations rapidly adopted systems like it to serve a wide spectrum of corporate processes. The corporation was still a nematode but we were wiring the worm and aggressively digitizing its nervous system.

Yet it remained basically the same worm. Sure, it became more efficient and could react faster but with basically the same dispositions, because as we automated those existing systems with computers we mimicked the paper. Invoices, accounts, and customer master files all simply migrated into the machine as we dumped file cabinets into database tables. We were wiring the worm, but we weren't re-wiring it.

So it remained a bureaucracy, just a more efficient, responsive, and scalable one. Yet this was the beginning of a symbiotic evolution between corporation and information age technology and it became a departure point in the corporation's further evolutionary history. This digital foundation is the substrate on which further evolutionary processes would occur.

Then about thirty years ago, Leonard Kleinrock, Lawrence Roberts, Robert Kahn, and Vint Cerf invented the Internet and ushered in the second epoch of information age, the network era.

Suddenly our little worm was connected to its peers and surrounding ecosystem in ways that it hadn't been before. Messaging between companies became as natural as messaging between desks and with later pushes by Jack Welch and others who understood the revolution that was at hand, those messages finally succumbed to the pull of digitization. The era of the paper purchase order and invoice finally died. The first 35 years of digitization had focused on internal processes; now the focus was more on interactions with the outside world. (I say more, because EDI had been around for a while. But it was with the cost structure of the Internet that it really took off.) For the worm it was like the evolution of a sixth sense. It could see further, predict deeper into the future, and respond faster.

But those new networks didn't just affect the way our corporations interacted with the outside world. They also began to erode the very foundation of bureaucracy: its hierarchy.

While the strict hierarchy of bureaucracy had been a force multiplier for labor during the industrial age, in practice it meant that a company could never be smarter than the smartest person at its head. Restrained by hierarchy, rigid rules, and specialized functions, the sum total of a corporation's intelligence was always much less than the sum of the intelligence of its participants.

With globalization, complex connections, and faster market cycle times the complexity of the corporation's environment has increased rapidly and has long since exceeded the complexity that any single person can understand. There has after all only been one Steve Jobs. Something had to give.

So corporations have (slowly) begun the journey toward more agile, network-enabled, learning organizations that can crowd source intelligence both within their ranks and from inside their customer bases. They are beginning to exhibit locally emergent behaviors in response to that learning. This is what is behind corporate mottos like Facebook's "Move fast and break stuff." It's just another way of saying that initiative is local and that the head can't know everything.

Of course companies in the network era still have organization charts. But they don't tell the whole story anymore. These days we need to analyze email patterns, phone records, instant messaging and other evidence of actual human connection to determine the real organizational model that emerges like an interstitial lattice within the official org chart.

So corporate evolution is no longer just incremental improvement along an efficiency and productivity vector. The very form of the corporation is changing, enabled by technology and spurred by the necessity of complexity and cycle times. The corporation is growing external sensors and the necessary neurons to deal with what it discovers. It is changing from dispositional and reactive to complex and emergent in order to better impedance match with the post-industrial world it occupies.

So here we are, at the doorstep of the Information Age's Big Data epoch. The corporation has already taken advantage of the computing and internet-working epochs to evolve significantly and adapt to a more complex world. But even bigger changes are ahead.

This book will take you through the entire Big Data story, so I'm not going to expound much on the meaning of Big Data here. I'll just describe enough to set the stage for the next phase of corporate evolution. And this is a key point: Big Data isn't Business Intelligence (BI) with bigger data.

We are no longer limited to the structured transactional world that has been the domain of corporate information technology for the last 55 years. Big Data represents a transition-in-kind for both storage and analysis. It isn't just about size.

The data your corporation does "BI" with today is mostly internally generated highly-structured transactional data. It's like a record of the neurons that fired. All too often the role of the business intelligence analyst really boils down to corporate kinesthesis. Reports are generated to tell the head of a hierarchy what its limbs are doing, or did.

But Big Data has the potential to be different. For one, often the data being analyzed will come from somewhere else, and in its original unstructured form. And two, we won't just be analyzing what we did; we'll be analyzing what is happening in the world around us, with all of the richness and detail of the original sensation.

Now we can think of web logs, video clips, voice response unit recordings, every document in every SharePoint repository, social data, open government data, partner data sets, and many more as part of our analytical corpus. No longer limited to mere introspection, analysis can be about more deeply detailed external sensing. What do my customers do? Who do they know? Were they happy or angry when they called? What are their network neighbors like and when and how much will they be influenced by them? Which of my customers are most similar? What are they saying about our competitors? What are they buying from our competitors? Are my competitors' parking lots full? And on and on…

Perhaps more importantly, how can this mass of data be turned directly into product, or at least an attribute of our products? Can we close the loop: from what we sense in our environment, to what to know, and to what we do?

The term data science speaks to the notion that we are now using data to apply the scientific method to our businesses. We create (or discover) hypotheses, run experiments, see if our customers react the way we predict and then build new products or interactions based on the results. Forward thinking companies are closing the loops so that the entire process runs without human intervention and products are updated in real time based on customer behavior or other inputs.

Put another way, the corporation's OODA Loop (Observe, Orient, Decide, Act. The work of USAF Col Boyd, the OODA loop describes a model for action in the face of uncertainty) is being implemented, at least in the tactical time scale, directly in the machinery of the corporation. Humans design the algorithms, but their participation isn't necessary beyond that. And unlike traditional BI, which focused on the OO of the OODA loop, the modern corporation has to directly integrate the Decide and Act phases to keep up with the dynamics of the modern market. It's not enough to be more analytical, future corporations will require greater product and organizational agility to act in real time.

As analogy, we humans experience our world in real time via internally rendered maps of our sensory perceptions, and we store those maps as memory. Maps are the scaffolding on which mind and our processes of self unfold. They are the evolutionary portal through which we passed from disposition to reasoning, when along the way we evolved from reactive worm to reasoning human.

By storing rich complex interactions, the corporation is beginning to create and store map-like structures as well. Instead of reducing complex interactions into the cartoonish renderings of summarized transactions, we are beginning to store the whole map, the pure bits from every sensor and touch point. And with the network and relationship data we are capturing now, corporate memories are beginning to look like the associative model of the human brain. The corporation isn't becoming a person, but it is becoming more than a worm. (I realize that as of this writing the Supreme Court disagrees with my assessment.) It's becoming intelligent.

The big data epoch will be one of a major transition. For the past 55 years the focus of information technology has been on wiring the worm for automation, efficiency, and productivity. Now I think we'll see that shift to support of the very intelligence of the corporation.

Until now we measured projects mostly on the ROI inherent in their potential cost savings. But we'll soon begin to think in terms of intelligentization—a made up word that means making something smarter. Our goal in business and IT will be the application of data and analytics to increasing corporate intelligence. Something like $IQ_{corp} = f(data, algorithms)$. That's an altogether different framing goal for technology, and it will mean new ways of organizing and conceptualizing how it is funded and delivered.

How does the data we capture and the algorithms we develop increase the intelligence of our organization? Can we begin to think in terms of something like an IQ for our companies—a combination of its sensory perception, recall, reasoning, and ability to act? Will we go from return on investment to acquisition of intelligence? Regardless, we will be building companies that are smarter and faster-reacting than the humans that run them.

Of course, this isn't the end of transactional IT. The corporation will have "vestigial IT" too just like the human brain still has regions remaining from our dispositional evolutionary past. After all, we still pull our hands away from a hot stove without thinking about it first, and companies will continue to automatically resupply empty shelves. But an intelligent corporation will be one with a seamlessly integrated post-dispositional reasoning mind wired for action. One that is more intelligent as a collection of people and as a set of systems than any member of its management, and one whose OODA loop often runs without human intervention.

Big Data is an epoch in the information age, and on the other side of this discontinuity in corporate evolution the companies you work for are going to be smarter.

JIM STOGDILL
General Manager, Radar, O'Reilly Media

PREFACE

Big Data, Big Analytics is written for business managers and executives who want to understand more about "Big Data." In researching this book, we realized that there were many texts about high-level strategy and some that went deep into the weeds with sample code. We have attempted to create a balance between the two, making the topic accessible through stories, metaphors, and analogies even though it's a technical subject area.

We've started out the book defining Big Data and discussing why Big Data is important. We illustrate the value of Big Data through industry examples in Chapter 2 and then move into describing the enabling technology in Chapters 3 through 5. While we introduce the people working with Big Data earlier in the book, in Chapter 6 we dive deeper into the organization and the roles it takes to make Big Data successful in an organization. We wrap up the book with a thorough summary of the ethical and privacy issues surrounding Big Data in Chapter 7. *Big Data, Big Analytics* concludes with an entertaining lecture by Avinash Kaushik of Google.

We welcome feedback. If you have ideas on how we can make this book better—or what topics you'd like covered in a new edition, we'd love to hear from you. Please visit us at www.BigDataBigAnalytics.com.

ACKNOWLEDGMENTS

We'd like to offer a special thanks to our extended team that helped us along the way: Stokes Adams, Mike Barlow, Sheck Cho, Stacey Rivera, and Paula Thorton.

We'd like to acknowledge the people and their organizations that have made helpful contributions to this book.

Chuck Alvarez	Morgan Stanley
Tasso Argyros	Teradata
Amr Awadallah	Cloudera
Ravi Bandaru	Nokia
Mike Barlow	Cumulus Partners
Randall Beard	Nielsen
David Botkin	Playdom
Nate Burns	State University of New York at Buffalo
David Champagne	Revolution Analytics
Drew Conway	IA Ventures
Joe Cunningham	Visa
Yves de Montcheiul	Talend
Anthony Deighton	QlikTech
Deepinder Dhingra	Mu Sigma
Zubin Dowlaty	Mu Sigma
Shaun Doyle	Cognitive Box
Michael Driscoll	Dataspora
Edd Dumbill	O'Reilly
John Elder	Elder Research
Usama Fayyad	Blue Kangaroo
Financial Services Team	CapGemini
Elissa Fink	Tableau Software
Chris Gage	John Wiley & Sons

Misha Ghosh	MasterCard Worldwide
Anthony Goldbloom	Kaggle
James Golden	Accenture
Pat Hanrahan	Tableau Software
Colin Hill	GNS Healthcare
Ben Hosken	FLINKLABS
Curtis Hougland	Attention
Josh James	Domo
Jeff Jonas	IBM
Avinash Kaushik	Google
Paul Kent	SAS
Dan Kerzner	Microstrategy
James Kobelius	IBM
Jared Lander	JP Lander Consulting
Steve Lucas	SAP
Creve Maples	Event Horizon
Jojy Matthew	Capgemini
Abhishek Mehta	Tresata
John Meister	MasterCard Worldwide
Jake Porway	DataKind
Ori Peled	MasterCard Worldwide
Murali Ramanathan	State University of New York at Buffalo
Andrew Reiskind	MasterCard Worldwide
Partha Sen	Fuzzy Logix
Giovanni Seni	Intuit
Niv Singer	Tracx
David Smith	Revolution Analytics
Dan Springer	Responsys
Jim Stogdill	O'Reilly
Marcia Tal	Tal Consulting
Ian Thomson	Ocean Crusaders

Paula Thornton	Independent Writer
Jer Thorp	New York Times
Nathan Yau	Student at UCLA
Michael Zeitlin	Aqumin

BIG DATA,
BIG ANALYTICS

Two men operating a mainframe computer, circa 1960. It's amazing how today's smartphone holds so much more data than this huge 1960's relic. (Photo by Pictorial Parade/Archive Photos)

CHAPTER 1

What Is Big Data and Why Is It Important?

Big Data is the next generation of data warehousing and business analytics and is poised to deliver top line revenues cost efficiently for enterprises. The greatest part about this phenomenon is the rapid pace of innovation and change; where we are today is not where we'll be in just two years and definitely not where we'll be in a decade.

Just think about all the great stories you will tell your grandchildren about the early days of the twenty-first century, when the Age of Big Data Analytics was in its infancy.

This new age didn't suddenly emerge. It's not an overnight phenomenon. It's been coming for a while. It has many deep roots and many branches. In fact, if you speak with most data industry veterans, Big Data has been around for decades for firms that have been handling tons of transactional data over the years—even dating back to the mainframe era. The reasons for this new age are varied and complex, so let's reduce them to a handful that will be easy to remember in case someone corners you at a cocktail party and demands a quick explanation of what's really going on. Here's our standard answer in three parts:

1. **Computing perfect storm.** Big Data analytics are the natural result of four major global trends: Moore's Law (which basically says that technology always gets cheaper), mobile computing (that smart phone or mobile tablet in your hand), social networking (Facebook, Foursquare, Pinterest, etc.), and cloud computing (you don't even have to own hardware or software anymore; you can rent or lease someone else's).

2. **Data perfect storm.** Volumes of transactional data have been around for decades for most big firms, but the flood gates have now opened with more *volume*, and the *velocity* and *variety*—the three Vs—of data that has arrived in unprecedented ways. This perfect storm of the three Vs makes it extremely complex and cumbersome with the current data management and analytics technology and practices.

3. **Convergence perfect storm.** Another perfect storm is happening, too. Traditional data management and analytics software and hardware technologies, open-source technology, and commodity hardware are merging to create new alternatives for IT and business executives to address Big Data analytics.

Let's make one thing clear. For some industry veterans, "Big Data" isn't new. There are companies that have dealt with billions of transactions for many years. For example, John Meister, group executive of Data Warehouse Technologies at MasterCard Worldwide, deals with a billion transactions on a strong holiday weekend. However, even the most seasoned IT veterans are awestruck by recent innovations that give their team the ability to leverage new technology and approaches, which enable us to affordably handle more data and take advantage of the variety of data that lives outside of the typical transactional world—such as unstructured data.

Paul Kent, vice president of Big Data at SAS, is an R&D professional who has developed big data crunching software for over two decades. At the SAS Global Forum 2012, Kent explained that the ability to store data in an affordable way has changed the game for his customers:

People are able to store that much data now and more than they ever before. We have reached this tipping point where they don't have to make decisions about which half to keep or how much history to keep. It's now economically feasible to keep all of your history and all of your variables and go back later when you have a new question and start looking for an answer. That hadn't been practical up until just recently. Certainly the advances in blade technology and the idea that Google brought to market of you take lots and lots of small Intel servers and you gang them together and use their potential in aggregate. That is the super computer of the future.

Let's now introduce Misha Ghosh, who is known to be an innovator with several patents under his belt. Ghosh is currently an executive at MasterCard Advisors and before that he spent 11 years at Bank of America solving business issues by using data. Ghosh explains, "Aside from the changes in the actual hardware and software technology, there has also been a massive change in the actual evolution of data systems. I compare it to the stages of learning: dependent, independent, and interdependent."

Using Misha's analogy, let's breakdown the three pinnacle stages in the evolution of data systems:

- **Dependent** (Early Days). Data systems were fairly new and users didn't know quite know what they wanted. IT assumed that "Build it and they shall come."
- **Independent** (Recent Years). Users understood what an analytical platform was and worked together with IT to define the business needs and approach for deriving insights for their firm.
- **Interdependent** (Big Data Era). Interactional stage between various companies, creating more social collaboration beyond your firm's walls.

Moving from independent (Recent Years) to interdependent (Big Data Era) is sort of like comparing Starbucks to a hip independent neighborhood coffee shop with wizard baristas that can tell you when the next local environmental advisory council meet-up is taking place. Both shops have similar basic product ingredients, but the independent neighborhood coffee shop provides an approach and atmosphere that caters to social collaboration within a given community. The customers share their artwork and tips about the best picks at Saturday's farmers market as they stand by the giant corkboard with a sea of personal flyers with tear off tabs . . . "Web Designer Available for Hire, 555-1302."

One relevant example and Big Data parity to the coffee shop is the New York City data meet-ups with data scientists like Drew Conway, Jared Lander, and Jake Porway. These bright minds organize meet-ups after work at places like Columbia University and NYU to share their latest analytic application [including a review of their actual code] followed by a trip to the local pub for a few pints and more data chatter. Their use cases are a blend of Big Data corporate applications and other applications that actually turn their data skills into a helping hand for humanity.

For example, during the day Jared Lander helps a large healthcare organization solve big data problems related to patient data. By night, he is helping a disaster recovery organization with optimization analytics that help direct the correct supplies to areas where they are needed most. Does a village need bottled water or boats, rice or wheat, shelter or toilets? Follow up surveys six, 12, 18, and 24 months following the disaster help track the recovery and direct further relief efforts.

Another great example is Jake Porway, who decided to go full time to use Big Data to help humanity at DataKind, which is the company he co-founded with Craig Barowsky and Drew Conway. From weekend events to long-term projects, DataKind supports a data-driven social sector through services, tools, and educational resources to help with the entire data pipeline.

In the service of humanity, they were able to secure funding from several corporations and foundations such as EMC, O'Reilly Media, Pop Tech, National Geographic, and the Alfred P. Sloan Foundation. Porway described DataKind to us as a group of data superheroes:

> I love superheroes, because they're ordinary people who find themselves with extraordinary powers that they use to make the world a better place. As data and technology become more ubiquitous and the need for insights more pressing, ordinary data scientists are finding themselves with extraordinary powers. The world is changing and those who are stepping up to use data for the greater good have a real opportunity to change it for the better.

In summary, the Big Data world is being fueled with an abundance mentality; a rising tide lifts all boats. This new mentality is fueled by a gigantic global corkboard that includes data scientists, crowd sourcing, and opens source methodologies.

A Flood of Mythic "Start-Up" Proportions

Thanks to the three converging "perfect storms," those trends discussed in the previous section, the global economy now generates unprecedented quantities of data. People who compare the amount of data produced daily to a deluge of mythic proportions are entirely correct. This flood of data represents something we've never seen before. It's new, it's powerful, and yes, it's scary but extremely exciting.

The best way to predict the future is to create it!

—Peter F. Drucker

The influential writer and management consultant Drucker reminds us that the future is up to us to create. This is something that every entrepreneur takes to heart as they evangelize their start-up's big idea that they know will impact the world! This is also true with Big Data and the new technology and approaches that have arrived at our doorstep.

Over the past decade companies like Facebook, Google, LinkedIn, and eBay have created treasured firms that rely on the skills of new data scientists, who are breaking the traditional barriers by leveraging new technology and approaches to capture and analyze data that drives their business. Time is flying and we have to remember that these firms were once start-ups. In fact, most of today's start-ups are applying similar Big Data methods and technologies while they're growing their businesses. The question is how.

This is why it is critical that organizations ensure that they have a mechanism to change with the times and not get caught up appeasing the ghost from data warehousing and business intelligence (BI) analytics of the past! At the end of the day, legacy data warehousing and BI analytics are not going away anytime soon. It's all about finding the right home for the new approaches and making them work for you!

According to a recent study by the McKinsey Global Institute, organizations capture trillions of bytes of information about their customers, suppliers, and operations through digital systems. Millions of networked sensors embedded in mobile phones, automobiles, and other products are continually sensing, creating, and communicating data. The result is a 40 percent projected annual growth in the volume of data generated. As the study notes, 15 out of 17 sectors in the U.S. economy already "have more data stored per company than the U.S. Library of Congress."[1] The Library of Congress itself has collected more than 235 terabytes of data. That's Big Data.

Big Data Is More Than Merely Big

What makes Big Data different from "regular" data? It really all depends on when you ask the question.

Edd Dumbill, founding chair of O'Reilly's Strata Conference and chair of the O'Reilly Open Source Convention, defines Big Data as "data that becomes large enough that it cannot be processed using conventional methods."

Here is how the McKinsey study defines Big Data:

> Big data refers to datasets whose size is beyond the ability of typical database software tools to capture, store, manage, and analyze. This definition is intentionally subjective. . . . We assume that, as technology advances over time, the size of datasets that qualify as big data will also increase. Also note that the definition can vary by sector, depending on what kinds of software tools are commonly available and what sizes of datasets are common in a particular industry. With those caveats, big data in many sectors today will range from a few dozen terabytes to multiple petabytes (thousands of terabytes).[2]

Big Data isn't just a description of raw volume. "The real issue is usability," according to industry renowned blogger David Smith. From his perspective, big datasets aren't even the problem. The real challenge is identifying or developing most cost-effective and reliable methods for extracting value from all the terabytes and petabytes of data now available. That's where Big Data analytics become necessary.

Comparing traditional analytics to Big Data analytics is like comparing a horse-drawn cart to a tractor–trailer rig. The differences in speed, scale, and complexity are tremendous.

Why Now?

On some level, we all understand that history has no narrative and no particular direction. But that doesn't stop us from inventing narratives and writing timelines complete with "important milestones." Keeping those thoughts in mind, Figure 1.1 shows a timeline of recent technology developments.

If you believe that it's possible to learn from past mistakes, then one mistake we certainly do not want to repeat is investing in new technologies that didn't fit into existing business frameworks. During the customer relationship management (CRM) era of the 1990s, many companies made substantial investments in customer-facing technologies that subsequently failed to deliver expected value. The reason for most of those failures was fairly straightforward: Management either forgot (or just didn't know) that big projects require a synchronized transformation of people, process, and technology. All three must be marching in step or the project is doomed.

We can avoid those kinds of mistakes if we keep our attention focused on the outcomes we want to achieve. The technology of Big Data is the easy part—the hard part is figuring out what you are going to do with the output generated by your Big Data analytics. As the ancient Greek philosophers said, "Action is character." It's what you do that counts. Putting it bluntly, make

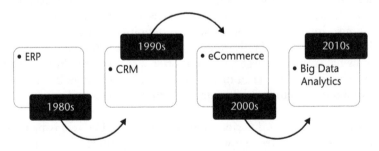

Figure 1.1 Timeline of Recent Technology Developments

sure that you have the people and process pieces ready before you commit to buying the technology.

A Convergence of Key Trends

Our friend, Steve Lucas, is the Global Executive Vice President and General Manager, SAP Database & Technology at SAP. He's an experienced player in the Big Data analytics space, and we're delighted that he agreed to share some of his insights with us. First of all, according to Lucas, it's important to remember that big companies have been collecting and storing large amounts of data for a long time. From his perspective, the difference between "Old Big Data" and "New Big Data" is accessibility. Here's a brief summary of our interview:

> Companies have always kept large amounts of information. But until recently, they stored most of that information on tape. While it's true that the amount of data in the world keeps growing, the real change has been in the ways that we access that data and use it to create value.
>
> Today, you have technologies like Hadoop, for example, that make it functionally practical to access a tremendous amount of data, and then extract value from it. The availability of lower-cost hardware makes it easier and more feasible to retrieve and process information, quickly and at lower costs than ever before.
>
> So it's the convergence of several trends—more data and less expensive, faster hardware—that's driving this transformation. Today, we've got raw speed at an affordable price. That cost/benefit has really been a game changer for us.
>
> That's first and foremost—raw horsepower. Next is the ability to do that real-time analysis on very complex sets of data and models, so it's not just let me look at my financials or let me look at marketing information. And finally, we now have the ability to find solutions for very complex problems in real time.

We asked Steve Lucas to offer some examples of scenarios in which the ability to analyze Big Data in real time is making an impact. Here's what he told us:

> A perfect example would be insurance companies. They need to know the answers to questions like this: As people age, what kinds of different services will they need from us?

In the past, the companies would have been forced to settle for general answers. Today, they can use their data to find answers that are more specific and significantly more useful. Here are some examples that Lucas shared with us from the insurance and retail industries:

> You don't have to guess. You can look at actual data, from real customers. You can extract and analyze every policy they've ever held. The answers to your questions are buried in this kind of massive mound of data—potentially petabytes worth of data if you consider all of your insurance customers across the lifespan of their policies. It's unbelievable how much information exists.
>
> But now you've got to go from the level of petabytes and terabytes down to the level of a byte. That's a very complex process. But today you can do it—you can compare one individual to all the other people in an age bracket and perform an analysis, in real time. That's pretty powerful stuff. Imagine if a customer service rep had access to that kind of information in real time. Think of all the opportunities and advantages there would be, for the company and for the customer.
>
> Here's another example: You go into a store to buy a pair of pants. You take the pants up to the cash register and the clerk asks you if you would like to save 10 percent off your purchase by signing up for the store's credit card.
>
> 99.9 percent of the time, you're going to say "no." But now let's imagine if the store could automatically look at all of my past purchases and see what other items I bought when I came in to buy a pair of pants—and then offer me 50 percent off a similar purchase? Now that would be relevant to me. The store isn't offering me another lame credit card—it's offering me something that I probably want, at an attractive price.

The two scenarios described by Lucas aren't fantasies. Yesterday, the cost of real-time data analysis was prohibitive. Today, real-time analytics have become affordable. As a result, market-leading companies are already using Big Data Analytics to improve sales revenue, increase profits, and do a better job of serving customers.

Before moving on, it's worth repeating that not all new Big Data technology is open source. For example, SAP successfully entered the Big Data market with SAP HANA, an in-memory database platform for real-time analytics and applications. Products like SAP HANA are reminders that suppliers of proprietary solutions, such as SAP, SAS, Oracle, IBM, and Teradata, are playing—and will obviously continue to play—significant roles in the evolution of Big Data analytics.

Relatively Speaking . . .

Big Data, as you might expect, is a relative term. Although many people define Big Data by volume, definitions of Big Data that are based on volume can be troublesome since some people define volume by the number of occurrences (in database terminology by the rows in a table or in analytics terminology known as the number of observations).

Some people define volume based on the number of interesting pieces of information for each occurrence (or in database terminology, the columns in a table or in analytics terminology the features or dimensions) and some people define volume by the combination of depth and width.

If you're a midmarket consumer packaged goods (CPG) company, you might consider 10 terabytes as Big Data. But if you're a multinational pharmaceutical corporation, then you would probably consider 500 terabytes as Big Data. If you're a three-letter government agency, anything less than a petabyte is considered small.

The industry has an evolving definition around Big Data that is currently defined by three dimensions:

1. Volume
2. Variety
3. Velocity

These are reasonable dimensions to quantify Big Data and take into account the typical measures around volume and variety plus introduce the velocity dimension, which is a key compounding factor.

Let's explore each of these dimensions further.

Data *volume* can be measured by the sheer quantity of transactions, events, or amount of history that creates the data volume, but the volume is often further exacerbated by the attributes, dimensions, or predictive variables. Typically, analytics have used smaller data sets called *samples* to create predictive models. Oftentimes, the business use case or predictive insight has been severely blunted since the data volume has purposely been limited due to storage or computational processing constraints. It's similar to seeing the iceberg that sits above the waterline but not seeing the huge iceberg that lies beneath the surface.

By removing the data volume constraint and using larger data sets, enterprises can discover subtle patterns that can lead to targeted actionable micro-decisions, or they can factor in more observations or variables into predictions that increase the accuracy of the predictive models. Additionally, by releasing the bonds on data, enterprises can look at data over a longer period of time to create more accurate forecasts that mirror real-world complexities of inter-related bits of information.

Data *variety* is the assortment of data. Traditionally data, especially operational data, is "structured" as it is put into a database based on the type of data (i.e., character, numeric, floating point, etc.). Over the past couple of decades, data has increasingly become "unstructured" as the sources of data have proliferated beyond operational applications.

Oftentimes, text, audio, video, image, geospatial, and Internet data (including click streams and log files) are considered *unstructured data*. However, since many of the sources of this data are programs the data is in actuality "semi-structured." Semi-structured data is often a combination of different types of data that has some pattern or structure that is not as strictly defined as structured data. For example, call center logs may contain *customer name + date of call + complaint* where the complaint information is unstructured and not easily synthesized into a data store.

Data *velocity* is about the speed at which data is created, accumulated, ingested, and processed. The increasing pace of the world has put demands on businesses to process information in real-time or with near real-time responses. This may mean that data is processed on the fly or while "streaming" by to make quick, real-time decisions or it may be that monthly batch processes are run interday to produce more timely decisions.

A Wider Variety of Data

The variety of data sources continues to increase. Traditionally, internally focused operational systems, such as ERP (enterprise resource planning) and CRM applications, were the major source of data used in analytic processing. However, in order to increase knowledge and awareness, the complexity of data sources that feed into the analytics processes is rapidly growing to include a wider variety of data sources such as:

- Internet data (i.e., clickstream, social media, social networking links)
- Primary research (i.e., surveys, experiments, observations)
- Secondary research (i.e., competitive and marketplace data, industry reports, consumer data, business data)
- Location data (i.e., mobile device data, geospatial data)
- Image data (i.e., video, satellite image, surveillance)
- Supply chain data (i.e., EDI, vendor catalogs and pricing, quality information)
- Device data (i.e., sensors, PLCs, RF devices, LIMs, telemetry)

The wide variety of data leads to complexities in ingesting the data into data storage. The variety of data also complicates the transformation (or the changing of data into a form that can be used in analytics processing) and analytic computation of the processing of the data.

The Expanding Universe of Unstructured Data

We spoke with Misha Ghosh to get a "level set" on the relationship between structured data (the kind that is easy to define, store, and analyze) and unstructured data (the kind that tends to defy easy definition, takes up lots of storage capacity, and is typically more difficult to analyze).

Unstructured data is basically information that either does not have a predefined data model and/or does not fit well into a relational database. Unstructured information is typically text heavy, but may contain data such as dates, numbers, and facts as well. The term *semi-structured data* is used to describe structured data that doesn't fit into a formal structure of data models. However, semi-structured data does contain tags that separate semantic elements, which includes the capability to enforce hierarchies within the data.

At this point, it's fair to ask: If unstructured data is such a pain in the neck, why bother? Here's where Ghosh's insight is priceless. Our conversation with him was long and wide-ranging, but here are the main takeaways that we would like to share with you:

- The amount of data (all data, everywhere) is doubling every two years.
- Our world is becoming more transparent. We, in turn, are beginning to accept this as we become more comfortable with parting with data that we used to consider sacred and private.
- Most new data is unstructured. Specifically, unstructured data represents almost 95 percent of new data, while structured data represents only 5 percent.
- Unstructured data tends to grow exponentially, unlike structured data, which tends to grow in a more linear fashion.
- Unstructured data is vastly underutilized. Imagine huge deposits of oil or other natural resources that are just sitting there, waiting to be used. That's the current state of unstructured data as of today. Tomorrow will be a different story because there's a lot of money to be made for smart individuals and companies that can mine unstructured data successfully.

The implosion of data is happening as we begin to embrace more open and transparent societies. "Résumés used to be considered private information," says Ghosh. "Not anymore with the advent of LinkedIn." We have similar stories with Instagram and Flickr for pictures, Facebook for our circle of friends, and Twitter for our personal thoughts (and what the penalty can be given the recent London Olympics, where a Greek athlete was sent home for violating strict guidelines on what athletes can say in social media).

"Even if you don't know how you are going to apply it today, unstructured data has value," Ghosh observes. "Smart companies are beginning to capture that value, or they are partnering with companies that can capture the value of unstructured data. For example, some companies use unstructured social data to monitor their own systems. How does that work? The idea is simple: If your customer-facing website goes down, you're going to hear about it really quickly if you're monitoring Twitter. Monitoring social media can also help you spot and fix embarrassing mistakes before they cost you serious money."

We know of one such "embarrassing mistake," when a large bank recently discovered that one of its ad campaigns included language that some people interpreted as hidden references to marijuana. The bank found out by monitoring social media.

Of course, not all unstructured data is useful. Lots of it is meaningless noise. Now is the time to begin developing systems that can distinguish between "%^*()334" and "your product just ate my carpet." In many ways, the challenges of Big Data and, in particular, unstructured data are not new. Distinguishing between signal and noise has been a challenge for time immemorial. The main difference today is that we are using digital technology to separate the wheat from the chafe. Companies like Klout have come up with influence scores that can be used to filter out pertinent data.

Talking to Misha Ghosh was a wake-up call. It's a reminder that now is the time to develop the experience that you will need later when the use of unstructured social data becomes commonplace and mainstream. In other words, learn as much as you can now, while there's still time to gain a competitive advantage, and before everyone else jumps on the bandwagon.

The growing demands for data volume, variety, and velocity have placed increasing demands on computing platforms and software technologies to handle the scale, complexity, and speed that enterprises now require to remain competitive in the global marketplace.

For a moment, let's forget about the definitions and technology underpinning Big Data analytics. Let's stop and ask the *big* question:

Is Big Data analytics worth the effort?

Yes, without a doubt Big Data analytics is worth the effort. It will be a competitive advantage, and it's likely to play a key role in sorting winners from losers in our ultracompetitive global economy.

Early validations of the business value are making their way into the public forum via leading technology research firms. For example, in December 2011, Nucleus Research concluded that analytics pays back $10.66 for every dollar spent, while Forrester produced a Total Economic Impact Report for IBM that concluded Epsilon realized a 222 percent ROI within 12 months from a combination of capital expenditure (capex) and operational expenditure (opex) savings, productivity increase plus a revenue lift of $2.54 million.[3,4] In another example, Nucleus Research determined that Media Math achieved a 212 percent in five months with an annual revenue lift of $2.2 million.[5]

And, yes, there will be business and technology hurdles to clear. From a business perspective, you'll need to learn how to:

- Use Big Data analytics to drive value for your enterprise that aligns with your core competencies and creates a competitive advantage for your enterprise
- Capitalize on new technology capabilities *and* leverage your existing technology assets
- Enable the appropriate organizational change to move towards fact-based decisions, adoption of new technologies, and uniting people from multiple disciplines into a single multidisciplinary team
- Deliver faster and superior results by embracing and capitalizing on the ever-increasing rate of change that is occurring in the global market place

Unlike past eras in technology that were focused on driving down operational costs mostly through automation, the "Analytics Age" has the potential to drive elusive top-line revenue for enterprises. For those enterprises that become adept with Big Data analytics, they will simultaneously minimize operational costs while driving top-line revenues to net substantial profit margins for their enterprise.

Big Data analytics uses a wide variety of advanced analytics, as listed in Figure 1.2, to provide:

- **Deeper insights.** Rather than looking at segments, classifications, regions, groups, or other summary levels you'll have insights into *all* the individuals, *all* the products, *all* the parts, *all* the events, *all* the transactions, etc.
- **Broader insights.** The world is complex. Operating a business in a global, connected economy is very complex given constantly evolving and changing conditions. As humans, we simplify conditions so we can process events and understand what is happening. But our best-laid plans often go astray because of the estimating or approximating. Big Data analytics takes into account all the data, including new data sources, to understand the complex, evolving, and interrelated conditions to produce more accurate insights.
- **Frictionless actions.** Increased reliability and accuracy that will allow the deeper and broader insights to be automated into systematic actions.

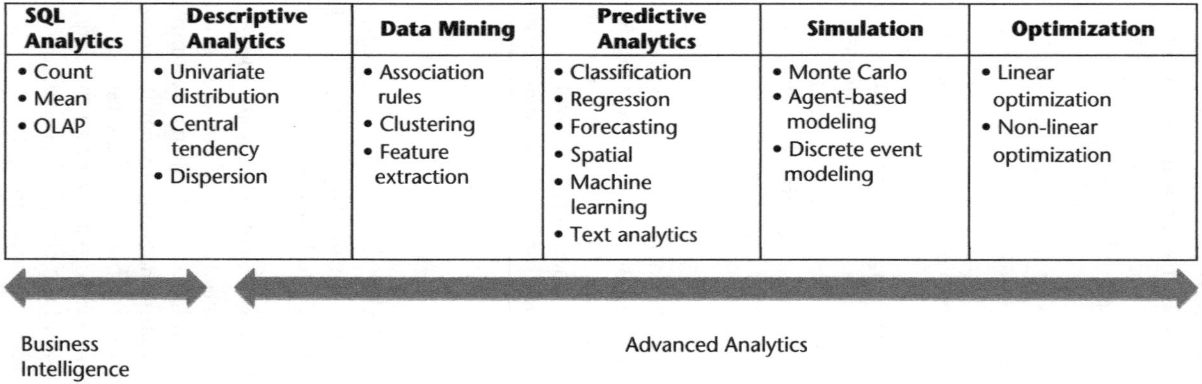

SQL Analytics	Descriptive Analytics	Data Mining	Predictive Analytics	Simulation	Optimization
• Count • Mean • OLAP	• Univariate distribution • Central tendency • Dispersion	• Association rules • Clustering • Feature extraction	• Classification • Regression • Forecasting • Spatial • Machine learning • Text analytics	• Monte Carlo • Agent-based modeling • Discrete event modeling	• Linear optimization • Non-linear optimization

Business Intelligence

Advanced Analytics

Figure 1.2 Analytics Spectrum

Table 1.1 Big Data Business Models

Improve Operational Efficiencies	Increase Revenues	Achieve Competitive Differentiation
Reduce risks and costs	Sell to microtrends	Offer new services
Save time	Enable self service	Seize market share
Lower complexity	Improve customer experience	Incubate new ventures
Enable self service	Detect fraud	

Source: Brett Sheppard, "Putting Big Data to Work: Opportunities for Enterprises," *GigaOm Pro,* March 2011.

GigaOm, a leading technology industry research firm, uses a simple framework (see Table 1.1) to describe potential Big Data Business Models for enterprises seeking to exploit Big Data analytics.

The competitive strategies outlined in the GigaOm framework are enabled today via packaged or custom analytic applications (see Table 1.2) depending on the maturity of the competitive strategy in the marketplace.

While Big Data analytics may not be the "Final Frontier," it certainly represents an enormous opportunity for businesses to exploit their data assets to realize substantial bottom line results for their enterprise. The key to success for organizations seeking to take advantage of this opportunity is:

- Leverage all your current data and enrich it with new data sources
- Enforce data quality policies and leverage today's best technology and people to support the policies
- Relentlessly seek opportunities to imbue your enterprise with fact-based decision making
- Embed your analytic insights throughout your organization

Setting the Tone at the Top

When mounting an argument for or against something, it's always a good idea to bring out your best minds. It's safe to say that Dr. Usama Fayyad is one of the best minds in Big Data analytics. A world-renowned pioneer in the world of analytics, data mining, and corporate data strategy, he was formerly Yahoo!'s chief data officer and executive vice president, as well as founder of Yahoo!'s research organization. A serial entrepreneur who founded his first startup, Audience Science (formerly DigiMine) in 2000 after leaving

Table 1.2 Enabling Big Data Analytic Applications

	Improve Operational Efficiencies	Increase Revenues	Achieve Competitive Differentiation
Mature Analytic Applications	■ Supply chain optimization ■ Marketing campaign optimization	■ Algorithmic trading	■ In-house custom analytic applications
Maturing Analytic Applications	■ Portfolio optimization ■ Risk management ■ Next best offer	■ Ad targeting optimization ■ Yield optimization	■ In-house custom analytic applications
Emerging Analytic Applications	■ Chronic disease prediction and prevention	■ Customer churn prevention	■ Product design optimization ■ Design of experiments optimization ■ Brand ■ Product Market Targeting

Microsoft, he sold his second company, DMX Group, to Yahoo! in 2004 and remained on Yahoo!'s senior executive team until late 2008. Prior to starting up ChoozOn, he was founder and CEO of Open Insights, a data strategy and data mining consulting firm working with the largest online and mobile companies in the world.

Dr. Fayyad's professional experience also includes five years at Microsoft directing the data mining and exploration efforts and developing database algorithms for Microsoft's Server Division. Prior to Microsoft he was with NASA's Jet Propulsion Laboratory, where he did award-winning work on the automated exploration of massive scientific databases. He earned his Ph.D. in engineering from the University of Michigan, Ann Arbor, and holds advanced degrees in electrical and computer engineering and in mathematics. He is also active in academic communities and is a Fellow of both the Association for Computing Machinery and the Association of the Advancement of Artificial Intelligence; he is Chairman of the ACM SIGKDD.

We include all of that biographical detail to make it clear that what Dr. Fayyad says really matters. In particular, his insights into the differences between traditional methods for handling data and newer methods are quite useful.

From his perspective, one of the most significant differences is that with Big Data analytics, you aren't constrained by predefined sets of questions or queries. With traditional analytics, the universe of questions you can ask the database is extremely small. With Big Data analytics, that universe is vastly larger. You can define new variables "on the fly." This is a very different scenario from the traditional methodologies, in which your ability to ask questions was severely limited.

Why is the ability to define new variables so critically important? The answer is easy: In the real world, you don't always know what you're looking for. So you can't possibly know in advance which questions you'll need to ask to find a solution.

Dr. Fayyad uses the second Palomar Sky Survey, a comprehensive effort to map the heavens, as an analogy to explain the inherent problems of handling Big Data. The survey, also known as POSS II, generated a huge amount of data. Here's a summary of what Dr. Fayyad told us in a recent interview:

> Astronomers are really, really good at extracting structure from image data. They think of the Sky Survey as a way of collecting layers of resolution data about billions of stars and other objects, which is very similar to how businesses deal with their customers. You know very little about the majority of your customers, and the data you have is noisy, incomplete, and potentially inaccurate. It's the same with stars.
>
> When the astronomers need to take a deeper look, they use a much higher resolution telescope that has a much narrower field of view of the sky. You're looking at a very tiny proportion of the universe, but you're looking much deeper, which means that you get much higher resolution data about those objects in the sky. When you have higher resolution data, a lot of objects that were hardly recognizable in the main part of the survey become recognizable. You can see whether they are stars or galaxies or something else.

Now the challenge becomes using what you've learned from one narrow sliver of the sky to predict what you will find in larger sections of the sky. Initially, the astronomers were working with 50 or 60 variables for each object. That's way too many variables for the human mind to handle. Eventually the astronomers discovered that only eight dimensions are necessary to make accurate predictions. Dr. Fayyad explains how this impacts the level of accuracy:

> They struggled with this problem for 30 years until they found the right variables. Of course, nobody knew that they needed only eight and they needed the eight simultaneously. Meaning, if you dropped

any one of the key attributes, it became very difficult to predict with better than 70 percent accuracy whether something was a star or a galaxy. But if you actually used all eight variables together, you could get up to the 90 to 95 percent level of accuracy level that's critical for drawing certain conclusions.

Nonscientific organizations, such as businesses and government agencies, face similar problems. Gathering data is often easier than figuring out how to use it. As the saying goes, "You don't know what you don't know." Are all of the variables important, or only a small subset? With Big Data analytics, you can get to the answer faster. Most of us won't have the luxury of working a problem for 30 years to find the optimal solution.

Notes

1. McKinsey Global Institute, "Big Data: The Next Frontier for Innovation, Competition, and Productivity," June 2011.
2. Ibid.
3. Nucleus Research, "Research Note: Analytics Pays Back $10.66 for Every Dollar Spent," Document L122, November 2011, http://nucleusresearch.com/research/notes-and-reports/analytics-pays-back-10-dot-66-for-every-dollar-spent/.
4. IBM Data Management and Forrester Consulting, "Total Economic Impact of IBM's Netezza Data Warehouse Appliance with Advanced Analytics," August 2011, http://ibmdatamag.com/2012/03/the-total-economic-impact-of-ibms-netezza-data-warehouse-appliance-with-advanced-analytics/.
5. Nucleus Research, ROI Case Study: IBM Smarter Commerce: Netezza MediaMath, Document L112, October 2011, www-01.ibm.com/software/success/cssdb.nsf/CS/JHUN-8N748A?OpenDocument&Site=default&cty=en_us.

CHAPTER 2

Industry Examples of Big Data

N
othing helps us understand Big Data more than examples of how the technology and approaches is being used in the "real world." Picking up on the concept of interdependency from Chapter 1, hopefully these examples help you think about how to apply ideas from other industries into your business.

Within this chapter you will read content that came from several thought leaders that we collected from thought leaders in subjects and industries such as Digital Marketing, Financial Services, Advertising, and Healthcare.

Digital Marketing and the Non-line World

Google's digital marketing evangelist and author Avinash Kaushik spent the first 10 years of his professional career in the world of business intelligence, during which he actually built large multiterabyte data warehouses and the intelligence platforms. In doing so, he learned how to help companies become more competitive with data. As Kaushik explains, he had to learn some hard and valuable lessons during this time:

> When I built data warehouses, one of the things we were constantly in quest of was these single sources of truth. My specialty was to work with large, complicated multinational companies and build the single source of truth in a relational database such as Oracle. The single source of truth would reply on very simplistic data from ERP and other sources.
>
> Now in hindsight the thing I had to learn quickly is that that the big data warehouse approach does not work in the online world. Back then we were tasked to collect all the clickstream data from our digital activities and it worked great for a few months, then it was a big disaster because everything that works in the BI world does not work in the online world. This is a painful lesson that I had to learn.

That led me to postulating this thing—that in order for you to be successful online, you have to *embrace multiplicity*. In fact, you have to give up on these deeply embedded principles that companies can survive by building a single source of the truth.

This multiplicity that Kaushik refers to requires multiple skills in the decision-making team, multiple tools, and multiple types of data (clickstream data, consumer data, competitive intelligence data, etc.). "The problem is that this approach and thinking is diametrically 100 percent opposed to the thing that we learned in the BI world," he says. "That's why most companies struggle with making smart decisions online because they cannot at some level, embrace multiplicity and they cannot bring themselves to embrace incomplete data and it is against their blood and DNA, they're forced to pick perfect data in order to make decisions."

Avinash Kaushik designed a framework in his book *Web Analytics 2.0: The Art of Online Accountability and Science of Customer Centricity*, in which he states that if you want to make good decisions on the Web, you have to learn how to use different kinds of tools to bring multiple types of data together and make decisions at the speed of light![1] As he told us, "You have to embrace incorrect data and make 80 percent good decisions every day and then not wait for the truth because by the time you get the truth, you're dead!"

Digital marketing encompasses using any sort of online media channel. It can be any existence online—whether profit or nonprofit—it doesn't matter. And it means driving people to a website, a mobile app, and the like, and, once there, retaining them, interacting with them. But digital marketing, too, has a material impact on what happens in the "offline," the real world according to Kaushik. A world his friend David Hughes calls the "non-line world":

The reality is that consumers live in a non-line world. They move fluidly between these two worlds. There is such little friction. When I'm in the offline world, I'm using my mobile phone or laptop to pull in information from the online world and vice versa. I'm taking snapshots now of coupons in the supermarket and then redeeming them online.

You can see how all of these experiences are coming together. I have very vehemently argued with companies that they need to think from an organizational perspective. Today they are organized to execute in an online world or an offline world. They need to organize for the non-line world. It has an implication of people, systems, marketing programs, data analysis. Non-line to me is this aspirational state where companies need to get to, but the truth is consumers are already there and have been for the last three to four years. It's as though some of us haven't caught up as companies in terms of how we think about our business and think about our data and how we think about executing a marketing program. Sometimes the inhibitor is about politics. That's why non-line marketing and non-line analytics are phrases that I end up using everywhere I go.

Avinash Kaushik describes a simplistic scenario involving a major newspaper publisher that struggled to find out with what people want to read when they come to their website or digital existence or mobile app or iPad app. One obvious action would be to have the analyst or the marketer log into Google analytics or Omniture's clickstream analysis tool and look at the top viewed pages on their website, mobile apps, and so on. That will help them understand what people want to read. Do they want to read more sports? International news? In their minds that will help frame the front page of the digital platform they have.

Kaushik then explains the actual reason for their problem: "The only way that your clickstream analysis tool can collect a piece of data is that a page has to be rendered, it executes the code for good analytics, and it records the page for you—now you know. But how will Google Analytics or Omniture actually measure the content that Karen [a name he gives a typical reader] wanted to read but could not find because you suck at the website navigation?"

In that scenario, there is no way that the publisher knows the content that Karen could not find because the page wasn't rendered. Kaushik elaborates:

> In order for you to actually find the data, one of the ways you would do it is you'd pop up a survey at the end of the visit by the person and you'd ask two different questions: Why are you here? Then they would ask you, were you able to complete your task? If the answer comes back to be no, it dynamically asks you what were you looking for.
>
> Then you would use that actual text by the user in order to understand what is it that people want that doesn't execute the code that would give the content that people really want. Then you have to bring these two pieces of disparate data together from two completely different systems—mash that massive data set together and then be smart enough to make a decision. This is what people actually want when they come to our website. Or this is what people were looking for, but we failed them.

That example may be simple, but the truth is digital marketing isn't easy. One facet is that corporations used to have all the data they needed for people who were their "consumers." They could do secondary research or some kind of primary research in order to collect data about people who might be prospective customers. That was all in their control. However, one of the problems we have to deal with in a Big Data, digital existence, is we do not have access to data for all our consumers. There is massive fragmentation as Kaushik describes:

> Again, the word multiplicity, in terms of how consumers interact with all the platforms they've created on the Web. We have only really good information about those people when they interact with our primary platforms, the ones we own, and we have very little information once they start to interact with us on other platforms—Facebook, Twitter, Google+, pick a platform. Then we have very little visibility about people when they meet in concentrated masses and talk about us, on platforms that are not ours in any way. We are starting to lose control of our ability to access the data we need in order to make smart, timely decisions.

Don't Abdicate Relationships

Many of today's marketers are discussing and assessing their approaches to engage consumers in different ways such as social media marketing. However, Avinash Kaushik believes that a lot of companies abdicate their primary online existence—their own websites—in favor of the company's Facebook page. For example, a large beer company urged consumers who came to the company's official website to go to Facebook where they could enter a sweepstakes. Without pulling any punches, Kaushik says, "It annoys the hell out of me. If you're going to be on Facebook, at least be great on Facebook . . . don't suck at it!"

When it comes to marketing, when it comes to consumer relationships, the thing that gets Kaushik excited is working with companies that never had the opportunity to have a relationship with a consumer directly because they abdicate, that is, they relinquish that relationship to their retailers. Now we've created this world where any company, no matter how far removed it is from a consumer can directly have a relationship with the consumer.

According to Kaushik, the companies that do this best are consumer package goods companies such as Proctor & Gamble (P&G). Now, for example, P&G can plug into the digital marketing world and get direct access to consumers through social media. Once that connection is made, it helps the firm with critical business decisions such as new product development. Kaushik advised this beer giant, with a multibillion-dollar marketing budget, to be on Facebook, but don't abdicate your own existence, your own outpost in the world because it's a lonely place where you can own the data about the consumers. He elaborated and explained:

You can engage consumers, understand who they are, collect your data, etc., and have a relationship with them, rather than a third party where you might have tertiary data; likes, fans, etc. In this case, you really have very little understanding of who those people are, how your marketing is working, how is it successful? Not successful? You don't know anything about it. I'm not saying they shouldn't have all these other outposts in the world, but what I'm saying is *you have to have the primary outpost from where you can collect your own "big data" and have a really solid relationship with the consumers you have and their data so you can make smarter decisions.*

Is IT Losing Control of Web Analytics?

Most people in the online publishing industry know how complex and onerous it could be to build an infrastructure to access and manage all the Internet data within their own IT department. Back in the day, IT departments would opt for a four-year project and millions of dollars to go that route. However, today this sector has built up an ecosystem of companies that spread the burden and allow others to benefit.

Avinash Kaushik believes there is one interesting paradigm shift that the Web mandates, that corporate information officers (CIOs) are and will continue to lose massive amounts of control over data and create large bureaucratic organizations whose only purpose is to support, collect, create, mash data, and be in the business of data "puking." He believes such CIOs are "losing control in spades":

> One of the interesting things that I had to grapple with as I embraced the Web and moved to the Web is that the primary way in which data gets collected, processed and stored, and accessed is actually at a third party. I did not have servers any more. I did not actually have implementations. I actually had to massively reduce the site of my implementation and data massaging and data serving and data banking team and rather massively expand the team that analyzes the data. This is the psychologically hard thing for me to do. When I was the BI person that's basically where most of the money of the company went. A little bit then went on analysts.

Kaushik's "elevator pitch" to businesses is that Big Data on the Web will completely transform a company's ability to understand the effectiveness of its marketing and hold its people accountable for the millions of dollars that they spend. It will also transform a company's ability to understand how its competitors are behaving. Kaushik believes that if you create a democracy in your organization where, rather than a few people making big decisions, the "organization is making hundreds and thousands of smart decisions every day and having the kind of impact on your company that would be impossible in the offline world. Not that the offline world is bad or anything, it's just that the way the data gets produced, assessed, and used on the Web is dramatically different."

Database Marketers, Pioneers of Big Data

We turned to database marketing guru Shaun Doyle for a brief history of the field, from its early days up to the present. Doyle is president and CEO of Cognitive Box, founded in 2002. Prior to setting up the company, he was vice president of Intelligent Marketing solutions at SAS. His primary areas of concentration were marketing automation solution and industry-specific solutions for the telecommunications and retail banking sectors.

During his time at SAS, Doyle founded and became chairman of Intrinsic, a campaign management vendor acquired by SAS in March 2001. Doyle is a genuinely brilliant database marketer, and our conversations with him covered a broad range of topics. Here's a brief summary of what he told us:

> Database marketing is really concerned with building databases containing information about individuals, using that information to better understand those individuals, and communicating effectively with some of those individuals to drive business value.
>
> Marketing databases are typically used for a couple of things. One thing is customer acquisition. There are some large-scale databases in the U.S. with large prospect universes and those prospect universes are used to acquire and drive incremental business. The second thing is retaining and cross-selling to existing customers, which reactivates the cycle.
>
> It began back in the 1960s, when people started building mainframe systems that contained information on customers and information about the products and services those customers were buying. People in marketing said, "Wait a minute, we can use that information to drive communications to those customers." In the '60s and early '70s, companies began extracting data from the mainframe, putting the data into separate databases, and then using those databases to drive direct mail activity.
>
> Back in those days, database marketing was predominantly direct mail. As companies grew and systems proliferated, we ended up with a situation where you had one system for one product, another system

for another product, and then potentially another system for another product. You had silos.

Then companies began developing technologies to manage and duplicate data from multiple source systems. Companies such as Acxiom and Experian started developing software that could eliminate duplicate customer information (de-duping). That enabled them to extract customer information from those siloed product systems, manage the information into a single database, remove all the duplicates, and then send direct mail to subsets of the customers in the database.

That's when database marketing really took off. Companies such as *Reader's Digest* and several of the larger financial services firms were early champions of this new kind of marketing, and they used it very effectively.

By the 1980s, marketers developed the ability to run reports on the information in their databases. The reports gave them better and deeper insights into the buying habits and preferences of customers. Companies began storing contact history, which enabled them to determine which kinds of direct-mail marketing campaigns generated the most responses and which kinds of customers were more likely to respond.

Telemarketing became popular when marketers figured out how to feed information extracted from customer databases to call centers. In the 1990s, email entered the picture, and marketers quickly saw opportunities for reaching customers via the Internet and the World Wide Web. As the dot-com boom accelerated, marketers rapidly adopted new technologies for pulling data from the web and using it to fuel online marketing campaigns. The Web also enabled marketers to launch campaigns based on behavioral data, and the promise of "real-time marketing" seemed just over the horizon.

Software vendors also saw an opportunity to sell marketing solutions directly to marketers. Most of the early database marketing was considered highly specialized work that was best handled by experts in bureaus that specialized in database marketing. The software vendors saw a new market and began developing products that didn't require highly specialized knowledge and post-graduate math skills to generate acceptable ROIs. Shaun Doyle explains how in the mid-1990s technology started to help marketers collect more relevant data to make informed decisions:

What happened next was that a number of companies began bringing these solutions in-house. Some companies stayed with the bureaus, but many became early adopters and began using new software for campaign management, reporting, and even predictive analytics.

Those newer tools were aimed specifically at the end-users, and by mid-90s, that whole trend had really gained momentum. There was a lot of new technology in the market, and as a result, companies started to do their own database marketing, in-house rather than externally.

The main advantage for the in-house approach is it enables you to bring in lots of different data from different places. We started to see detailed data based on a product, detailed transactional data; in the case of banks, they saw detailed data about individual transactions within bank accounts.

Companies started collecting information from customer care centers. The data became richer, creating a better picture of the individual and the mix of products and services that purchased. We had much better sets of data around who's contacting whom.

Thanks to all of this, we started to see significant business benefits coming from database marketing. If you ran a direct mail company and you used predictive analytics to the bottom 20 percent, that represented a direct savings in performance. Database marketing really entered its heyday, and then it got even better.

As technology improved, we saw the adoption of HTML email, which led directly to a spike in the use of email marketing. Now we could use color imagery. We could also facilitate a call to action, because somebody clicked on a link in an email, it would take them to a website where they'd be able to purchase a product.

By the late 1990s, proactive communication was the hot trend in marketing. The arrival of newer and more effective marketing automation solutions accelerated the trend. The term *marketing automation* refers to software platforms designed to automate repetitive tasks in critical areas such as campaign management. Doyle explains how that helped the marketers in today's world of Big Data:

Marketing automation technologies made it possible to drive what we called "timing around communication." In the old days, when we pulled the list, it could take anywhere from weeks to three months before the direct mail piece landed on your doorstep. In the 90s we saw the process reduced to a couple of days, and in the case of email, we could execute almost in real-time. That meant that messages directed to the consumers could be richer, more timely, more relevant, and more engaging.

In the 1990s, we also began seeing signs of scale emerging. Databases got larger and larger. We also saw the credit card companies, the early adopters of database marketing, creating prospect universes. Now you could have a database that contained every household in the U.S.—the total universe of prospects, in one place. Instead of having 10 million customers in a database, they had 260 million people.

As technology evolved to absorb greater volumes of data, the costs of data environments started to come down, and companies began collecting even more transactional data. That transactional data was used to drive more database activity, which in turn generated significantly higher volumes of transactional data.

As more industries (retail, insurance, consumer credit, automotive, pharmaceutical) saw the value of database marketing, the trend continued accelerating. Now we had really rich data, and that led to richer data analytics.

In the past five years, we've seen exponential growth in database marketing. Avis is a great example of that. They have a single database that has everybody that's rented a car, globally. The sheer scale of the volume of data is truly amazing.

And that new scale is pushing up against the limits of technology. As a result, we're seeing lots of innovation and new approaches. We're seeing new capabilities like offer optimization and real-time data warehousing, and greater use of real-time communication technologies. We're now getting to the point where we actually know more about you than you probably realize.

Today, many companies have the capability to store and analyze data generated from every search you run on their websites, every article you read, and every product you look at. By combining that specific data with anonymous data from external sources, they can predict your likely behavior with astonishing accuracy. It might sound creepy, but it's also helping keep us safe from criminals and terrorists. "A lot of the technology used by the CIA and other security agencies evolved through database marketing," says Doyle. "And some of the tools originally developed for database marketers are now used to detect fraud and prevent money-laundering."

Big Data and the New School of Marketing

Dan Springer, CEO of Responsys, defines the new school of marketing: "Today's consumers have changed. They've put down the newspaper, they fast forward through TV commercials, and they junk unsolicited email. Why? They have new options that better fit their digital lifestyle. They can choose which marketing messages they receive, when, where, and from whom. They prefer marketers who talk with them, not at them. New School marketers deliver what today's consumers want: relevant interactive communication across the digital power channels: email, mobile, social, display and the web."

Consumers Have Changed. So Must Marketers.

While using a lifecycle model is still the best way to approach marketing, today's new cross-channel customer is online, offline, captivated, distracted, satisfied, annoyed, vocal, or quiet at any given moment. The linear concept of a traditional funnel, or even a succession of lifecycle "stages," is no longer a useful framework for planning marketing campaigns and programs.

Today's cross-channel consumer is more dynamic, informed, and unpredictable than ever. Marketers must be ready with relevant marketing at a moment's notice. Marketing to today's cross-channel consumer demands a more nimble, holistic approach, one in which customer behavior and preference data determine the content and timing—and delivery channel—of marketing messages. Marketing campaigns should be cohesive: content should be versioned and distributable across multiple channels. Marketers should collect holistic data profiles on consumers, including channel response and preference data, social footprint/area of influence, and more. Segmentation strategies should now take into account channel preferences.

Marketers can still drive conversions and revenue, based on their own needs, with targeted campaigns sent manually, but more of their marketing should be driven by—and sent via preferred channels in response to—individual customer behaviors and events. How can marketers plan for that? Permission, integration, and automation are the keys, along with a more practical lifecycle model designed to make every acquisition marketing investment result in conversion, after conversion, after conversion.

The Right Approach: Cross-Channel Lifecycle Marketing

Cross-Channel Lifecycle Marketing really starts with the capture of customer permission, contact information, and preferences for multiple channels. It also requires marketers to have the right integrated marketing and customer information systems, so that (1) they can have complete understanding of customers through stated preferences and observed behavior at any given time; and (2) they can automate and optimize their programs and processes throughout the customer lifecycle. Once marketers have that, they need a practical framework for planning marketing activities. Let's take a look at the various loops that guide marketing strategies and tactics in the Cross-Channel Lifecycle Marketing approach: conversion, repurchase, stickiness, win-back, and re-permission (see Figure 2.1).

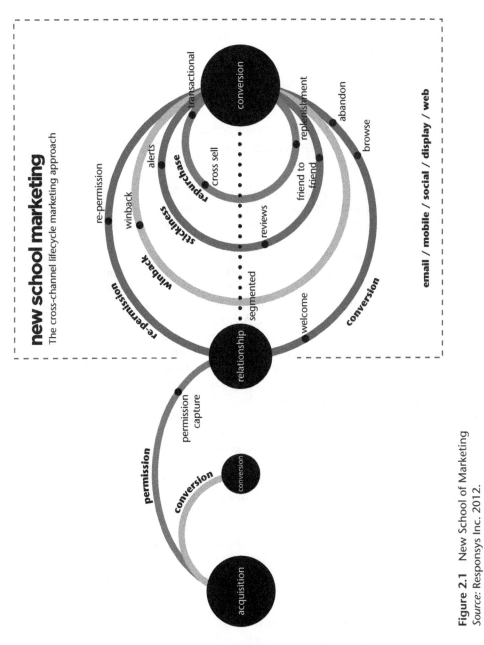

Figure 2.1 New School of Marketing
Source: Responsys Inc. 2012.

Social and Affiliate Marketing

The Avon Lady has been doing it for over a century. Tupperware parties made buying plastics acceptable back in the 1940s. Word-of-mouth marketing has been the most powerful form or marketing since before the Internet was an idea in Tim Berners-Lee's mind and well before Mark Zuckerberg ever entered that now-famous Harvard dorm room.

> *It's really just a VERY big Tupperware party.*
> — Greg Doran, Founder and CEO of TipSpring

What Berners-Lee's and Zuckerberg's ground-breaking concepts and inventions do for word-of-mouth marketers is provide a backbone to bring proven marketing concepts outside of the living room to a scale never before seen.

The concept of affiliate marketing, or pay for performance marketing on the Internet is often credited to William J. Tobin, the founder of PC Flowers & Gifts. In the early 1990s Tobin was granted patents around the concept of an online business rewarding another site (an affiliate site) for each referred transaction or purchase. Amazon.com launched its own affiliate program in 1996 and middleman affiliate networks like Linkshare and Commission Junction emerged preceding the 1990s Internet boom, providing the tools and technology to allow any brand to put affiliate marketing practices to use. Today, one would be hard pressed to find a major brand that does not have a thriving affiliate program. Today, industry analysts estimate affiliate marketing to be a $3 billion industry. It's an industry that largely goes anonymous. Unlike email and banner advertising, affiliate marketing is a behind the scenes channel most consumers are unaware of.

In 2012, the emergence of the social web brings these concepts together. What only professional affiliate marketers could do prior to Facebook, Twitter, and Tumblr, now any consumer with a mouse can do. Couponmountain.com and other well know affiliate sites generate multimillion dollar yearly revenues for driving transactions for the merchants they promote. The expertise required to build, host, and run a business like Couponmountain.com is no longer needed when a consumer with zero technical or business background can now publish the same content simply by clicking "Update Status" or "Tweet." The barriers to enter the affiliate marketing industry as an affiliate no longer exist.

Above and beyond the removal of barriers the social web brings to affiliate marketing, it also brings into the mix the same concepts behind the Avon Lady and Tupperware party—product recommendations from a friend network. As many detailed studies have shown, most people trust a recommendation from the people they know. While professional affiliate marketing sites provide the aggregation of many merchant offers on one centralized site, they completely lack the concept of trusted source recommendations.

Using the backbone and publication tools created by companies like Facebook and Twitter, brands will soon find that rewarding their own consumers for their advocacy is a required piece of their overall digital marketing mix. What's old is new again. While not every company in the past had the resources or knowhow to build an army of Avon Ladies, today there is no excuse. The tools are available to them all and the scale is exponentially larger than ever before. Anyone can recommend a product through the click of a mouse. No more parties needed.

Empowering Marketing with Social Intelligence

We also spoke with Niv Singer, Chief Technology Officer at Tracx, a social media intelligence software provider. Niv had quite a bit to say about the big data challenges faced in the social media realm and how it's impacting the way business is done today—and in the future.

As a result of the growing popularity and use of social media around the world and across nearly every demographic, the amount of user-generated content—or "big data"—created is immense, and continues growing exponentially. Millions of status updates, blog posts, photographs, and videos are shared every second. Successful organizations will not only need to identify the information relevant to their company and products—but also be able to dissect it, make sense of it, and respond to it—in real time and on a continuous basis, drawing business intelligence—or insights—that help predict likely future customer behavior. And if that sounds like a tall and complex order, that's because it is. Singer explains how this can be a challenging:

> It can sometimes be a real challenge to unify social profiles for a single user who may be using different names or handles on each of their social networks, so we've built an algorithm that combs through key factors including content of posts, and location, among others, to provide a very robust identity unification.

This brings us to the topic of influence and the age old debate of "who is an influencer?" To some brands, influence is measured purely by reach and to others, true influence is more of a function of quality and thoughtfulness of posts showing a real understanding of a given topic, and yet others gauge influence via social engagement or conversations. Because influence is so subjective, Singer believes the client should have the flexibility to sort influencers by any of these characteristics:

Very intelligent software is required to parse all that social data to define things like the sentiment of a post. We believe using a system that's also able to learn over time what that sentiment means to a specific client or brand and then represent that data with increased levels of accuracy provides clients a way to "train" a social platform to measure sentiment more closely to the way they would be doing it manually themselves. We also know it's important for brands to be able to understand the demographic information of the individual driving social discussions around their brand such as gender, age, and geography so they can better understand their customers and better target campaigns and programs based on that knowledge.

In terms of geography, Singer explained that they are combining social check-in data from Facebook, Foursquare, and similar social sites and applications over maps to show brands at the country, state/region, state, and down to the street level where conversations are happening about their brand, products, or competitors. This capability enables marketers with better service or push coupons in real time, right when someone states a need, offering value, within steps from where they already are, which has immense potential to drive sales and brand loyalty.

These challenges are in the forefront of technology, but also require very creative people and solutions. Every component in the system must be able to be distributed across multiple servers that don't rely on each other. No single point of failure is allowed—the data must therefore be replicated and stored on different machines, but should still be consistent. The data is later accessed in unpredictable ways. Singer likes to use an analogy to a book in a library:

> Finding a book by title or ISBN number is easy, even in a very big library. Finding, or counting, all the books written by specific authors is also relatively easy. It gets a little more complicated when we try to locate all the books written in a certain year, since we usually keep the books on shelves and sort them according to the author. If we need to count the number of books that contain the word "data" in their title written every year, it gets even more complicated. . . and when we need to locate all the books that contain the phrase "big data" in them, well, you can imagine.

Fundamentally, Singer doesn't view social data as a silo and, instead, believes that the real power comes in mining social data for business intelligence, not only for marketing, but also for customer support and sales. As a result, they've created a system from the ground up that was architected to be open. It's designed to be a data management system that just happens to be focused on managing unstructured social data, but we can easily integrate with other kinds of data sets. It was built with the expectation that social data would not live in an island, but would be pushed out to other applications to provide added business value and insights and that they would be pulling external data in.

This open approach like Singer is suggesting is extremely important because it enables businesses to take action with the data! Examples include integration with CRM systems like Salesforce.com and Microsoft Dynamics to enable companies to get a more holistic view of what's going with their clients by supplementing existing data sets that can be more static in nature with the social data set, which is more dynamic and real-time. Another example is integration with popular analytics platforms like Google Analytics and Omniture, so marketers can see a direct correlation and payoff of social campaigns through improved social sentiment or an increase in social conversations around their brand or product.

Where does Singer think this is all headed next? To the next big holy grail: an ability to take all this unstructured data and identify a customer's intent to buy:

> Customer intent is the big data challenge we're focused on solving. By applying intelligent algorithms and complex logic with very deep, real-time text analysis, we're able to group customers in to buckets such as awareness, opinion, consideration, preference and purchase. That ability let's marketers create unique messages and offers for people along each phase of the purchase process and lets sales more quickly identify qualified sales prospects.

One of Tracx customers is Attention, a heavily data-driven social media marketing agency also based in NYC. The Attention team uses the platform as the backbone of their social market research. Attention's CEO and Founder, Curtis Hougland, had this to say about Big Data's impact on marketing:

> Social media is the world's largest and purest focus group. Marketers now have the opportunity to mine social conversations for purchase intent and brand lift through Big Data. So, marketers can communicate with consumers when they are emotionally engaged, regardless of the channel. Since this data is captured in real-time, Big Data is coercing marketing organizations into moving more quickly to optimize media mix and message as a result of these insights. Since this data sheds light on all aspects of consumer behavior, companies are eliminating silos within the organization to align data to insight to prescription across channels, across media, and across the path to purchase. The days of Don Draper are over, replaced by a union of creative and quant.

The capability to understand a customer's intent that Hougland and Singer are referring to is not only good for the corporations; it's also a helpful capability for the client too. Think about it, most people communicate socially because they are looking to share, complain, or find something they need. Wouldn't it be great if someone was listening and knew your intent so that they can provide customer assistance or get you what you need for the best price?

Fraud and Big Data

Fraud is intentional deception made for personal gain or to damage another individual. One of the most common forms of fraudulent activity is credit card fraud. The credit card fraud rate in United States and other countries is increasing. As per Javelin's research, "8th Annual Card Issuers' Safety Scorecard: Proliferation of Alerts Lead to Quicker Detection Time and Lower Fraud Costs," credit card fraud incidence increased 87 percent in 2011 culminating in an aggregate fraud loss of $6 billion.[2] However, despite the significant increase in incidence, total cost of credit card fraud increased only 20 percent. The comparatively small rise in total cost can be attributed to an increasing sophistication of fraud detection mechanisms. According to the Capgemini Financial Services Team:

> Even though fraud detection is improving, the rate of incidents is rising. This means banks need more proactive approaches to prevent fraud. While issuers' investments in detection and resolution has resulted in an influx of customer-facing tools and falling average detection times among credit card fraud victims, the rising incidence rate indicates that credit card issuers should prioritize preventing fraud.
>
> Social media and mobile phones are forming the new frontiers for fraud. Despite warnings that social networks are a great resource for fraudsters, consumers are still sharing a significant amount of personal information frequently used to authenticate a consumer's identity. Those with public profiles (those visible to everyone) were more likely to expose this personal information.

According to Javelin's "2012 Identity Fraud Report: Social Media and Mobile Forming the New Fraud Frontier," 68 percent of people with public social media profiles shared their birthday information (with 45 percent sharing month, date, and year); 63 percent shared their high school name; 18 percent shared their phone number; and 12 percent shared their pet's name—all are prime examples of personal information a company would use to verify your identity.[3]

In order to prevent the fraud, credit card transactions are monitored and checked in near real time. If the checks identify pattern inconsistencies and suspicious activity, the transaction is identified for review and escalation.

The Capgemini Financial Services team believes that due to the nature of data streams and processing required, Big Data technologies provide an optimal technology solution based on the following three Vs:

1. **High volume.** Years of customer records and transactions (150 billion+ records per year)
2. **High velocity.** Dynamic transactions and social media information
3. **High variety.** Social media plus other unstructured data such as customer emails, call center conversations, as well as transactional structured data

Capgemini's new fraud Big Data initiative focuses on flagging the suspicious credit card transactions to prevent fraud in near real-time via multi-attribute monitoring. Real-time inputs involving transaction data and customers records are monitored via validity checks and detection rules. Pattern recognition is performed against the data to score and weight individual transactions across each of the rules and scoring dimensions. A cumulative score is then calculated for each transaction record and compared against thresholds to decide if the transaction is potentially suspicious or not.

The Capgemini team pointed out that they use an open-source weapon named Elastic Search, which is a distributed, free/open-source search server based on Apache Lucene (see Figure 2.2). It can be used to search all kind of documents at near real-time. They use the tool to index new transactions, which are sourced in real-time, which allows analytics to run in a distributed fashion utilizing the data specific to the index. Using this tool, large historical data sets can be used in conjunction with real-time data to identify deviations from typical payment patterns. This Big Data component allows overall historical patterns to be compared and contrasted, and allows the number of attributes and characteristics about consumer behavior to be very wide, with little impact on overall performance.

Once the transaction data has been processed, the percolator query then performs the functioning of identifying new transactions that have raised profiles. *Percolator* is a system for incrementally processing updates to large data sets. Percolator is the technology that Google used in building the index—that links keywords and URLs—used to answer searches on the Google page.

Percolator query can handle both structured and unstructured data. This provides scalability to the event processing framework, and allows specific suspicious transactions to be enriched with additional unstructured

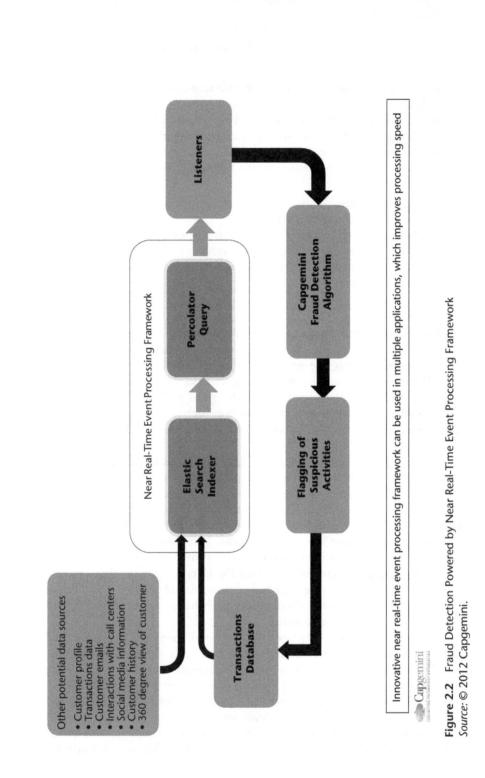

Figure 2.2 Fraud Detection Powered by Near Real-Time Event Processing Framework
Source: © 2012 Capgemini.

information—phone location/geospatial records, customer travel schedules, and so on. This ability to enrich the transaction further can reduce false-positives and increase the experience of the customer while redirecting fraud efforts to actual instances of suspicious activity.

Another approach to solving fraud with Big Data is social network analysis (SNA). SNA is the precise analysis of social networks. Social network analysis views social relationships and makes assumptions. SNA could reveal all individuals involved in fraudulent activity, from perpetrators to their associates, and understand their relationships and behaviors to identify a bust out fraud case.

According to a recent article in bankersonline.com posted by Experian, "bust out" is a hybrid credit and fraud problem and the scheme is typically defined by the following behavior:

- The account in question is delinquent or charged-off.
- The balance is close to or over the limit.
- One or more payments have been returned.
- The customer cannot be located.
- The above conditions exist with more than one account and/or financial institution.[4]

There are some Big Data solutions in the market like SAS's SNA solution, which helps institutions and goes beyond individual and account views to analyze all related activities and relationships at a network dimension. The network dimension allows you to visualize social networks and see previously hidden connections and relationships, which potentially could be a group of fraudsters. Obviously there are huge reams of data involved behind the scene, but the key to SNA solutions like SAS's is the visualization techniques for users to easily engage and take action.

Risk and Big Data

Many of the world's top analytics professionals work in risk management. It would be an understatement to say that risk management is data-driven—without advanced data analytics, modern risk management would simply not exist. The two most common types of risk management are credit risk management and market risk management. A third type of risk, operational risk management, isn't as common as credit and market risk.

The tactics for risk professionals typically include avoiding risk, reducing the negative effect or probability of risk, or accepting some or all of the potential consequences in exchange for a potential upside gain.

Credit risk analytics focus on past credit behaviors to predict the likelihood that a borrower will default on any type of debt by failing to make payments which they obligated to do. For example, "Is this person likely to default on their $300,000 mortgage?"

Market risk analytics focus on understanding the likelihood that the value of a portfolio will decrease due to the change in stock prices, interest rates, foreign exchange rates, and commodity prices. For example, "Should we sell this holding if the price drops another 10 percent?"

Credit Risk Management

Credit risk management is a critical function that spans a diversity of businesses across a wide range of industries. Ori Peled is the American Product Leader for MasterCard Advisors Risk & Marketing Solutions. He brings several years of information services experience in his current role with MasterCard and having served in various product development capacities at Dun & Bradstreet. Peled shares his insight with us on credit risk:

> Whether you're a small B2B regional plastics manufacturer or a large global consumer financial institution, the underlying credit risk principles are essentially the same: driving the business using the optimal balance of risk and reward.

Traditionally, credit risk management was rooted in the philosophy of minimizing losses. However, over time, credit risk professionals and business leaders came to understand that there are acceptable levels of risk that can boost profitability beyond what would normally have been achieved by simply focusing on avoiding write-offs. The shift to the more profitable credit risk management approach has been aided in large part to an ever-expanding availability of data, tools, and advanced analytics.

Credit risk professionals are stakeholders in key decisions that address all aspects of a business, from finding new and profitable customers to maintaining and growing relationships with existing customers. Maximizing the risk and reward opportunities requires that risk managers understand their customer portfolio, allowing them to leverage a consistent credit approach while acknowledging that you can't treat every customer the same.

As businesses grow, what starts out as a manual and judgmental process of making credit decisions gives way to a more structured and increasingly automated process in which data-driven decisions becomes the core. Decisions that impact not only revenue but also operational costs like staffing levels of customer support representatives or collections agents.

The vast amount of both qualitative and quantitative information available to credit risk professionals can be overwhelming to digest and can slow down a process with potential sales at risk. With advanced analytical tools, these abundant and complex data sources can be distilled into simple solutions that provide actionable insights and are relatively easy to implement. As an example, credit scoring solutions allow risk managers to apply a credit policy more efficiently and consistently across the business. Scoring solutions can take various data sources and produce a score that computes the odds of a customer behaving in a specific way. Traditional scoring methods focus on predicting the likelihood of delinquency or bankruptcy but additional scoring solutions can also help companies identify the profitability potential of customers or from a marketing perspective, the propensity to spend. Additionally, companies are leveraging and combining multiple analytical solutions at the same time—this could be a combination of proprietary scoring solutions and third party scoring like those provided by specialized analytics providers and the consumer and commercial bureaus (e.g., Experian, Equifax, D&B, etc.).

As you look across the credit risk management lifecycle, rich data sources and advanced analytics are instrumental throughout. From a customer acquisition perspective, credit risk managers decide whether to extend credit and how much. Lacking any previous experience with the prospect, they depend heavily on third-party credit reports and scores and may assist marketing organizations in employing customized look-alike models to help identify prospective best customers.

From an existing customer standpoint, the focus shifts to ongoing account management and retaining profitable accounts. This requires periodic customer risk assessments that influence key decisions on credit line increases and decreases. Again, advanced analytical solutions come into play, especially in larger organizations where the volume of accounts dictate a need for automated decisioning solutions that leverage behavior scores and other data sources. Continuous monitoring of an existing portfolio can also help credit risk managers forecast expected losses and better manage their collections efforts. Advanced analytics in the collections phase can help identify customers most likely to pay or even respond to different collection strategies and approaches.

The future of credit risk management will continue to change as we leverage new data sources emanating from a highly digital and mobile world. As an example, social media and cell phone usage data are opening up new opportunities to uncover customer behavior insights that can be used for credit decisioning. This is especially relevant in the parts of the world where a majority of the population is unbanked and traditional bureau data is unavailable.

As Figure 2.3 illustrates, there are four critical parts of the typical credit risk framework: planning, customer acquisition, account management, and collections. All four parts are handled in unique ways through the use of Big Data.

Figure 2.3   Credit Risk Framework
Source: Ori Peled.

Big Data and Algorithmic Trading

Partha Sen is the CEO of Fuzzy Logix, a company that specializes in high-performance, cross platform in database, and GPU (graphics processing unit) analytics. Sen spent over 15 years as a quantitative analyst in the financial services industry. Over the course of his career, he developed over 700 highly parallelized algorithms in C/C. He, along with a team of very talented quantitative professionals, now leverages his formidable expertise to help customers across a number of industries.

Sen has seen a significant shift in the use of data in the financial services industry over the past decade. "Financial institutions," he says, "particularly investment banks, have been at the forefront of applying analytics for risk management, proprietary trading, and portfolio management."

As most of you know, many investment banks use algorithmic trading, a highly sophisticated set of processes in which "insights" are made "actionable" via automated "decisions." Algorithmic trading relies on sophisticated mathematics to determine buy and sell orders for equities, commodities, interest rate and foreign exchange rates, derivatives, and fixed income instruments at blinding speed. A key component of algorithmic trading is determining return and the risk of each potential trade, and then making a decision to buy or sell. Quantitative risk analysts help banks develop trading rules and implement these rules using modern technology. Algorithmic trading involves a huge number of transactions with complex interdependent data, and every millisecond matters.

It's fair to say that these days banks focus more closely on market risk today than ever before. Market risk is basically the risk due to a fluctuation in the value of assets in the marketplace. For a given portfolio, you are trying to determine the probability that the value of the portfolio will fall within a certain threshold within five days, within seven days, within one month. With asset volatilities as high as they have been observed in the last few years, a lot of stress is being put on market risk. Sophisticated methods for managing market risk depend very heavily of modern technology.

Apart from investment banks, corporate and retail banks also rely very heavily on quantitative techniques. Two areas that readily come to mind are marketing, where they solicit households for financial products like credit cards, and credit risk management, where banks try to understand the probability that borrowers will default on loan. The models used in these areas for future outcomes are created with huge number of variables. For example, a model of the default risk for credit cards could be influenced by demographic factors, whether people have a job or not, what is the growth in the economy, and interest rates. There can be hundreds of factors or variables for each credit card. A typical retail bank will evaluate somewhere north of 5,000 factors for one given model to establish or calculate the probability of each of the borrowers defaulting. The number of calculations just for the risk factor can easily climb into *billions of calculations* being performed to calculate risk for a portfolio.

Crunching Through Complex Interrelated Data

In a frictionless economy, time is the critical driver to gain and sustain a competitive advantage. Every second, or more correctly, every millisecond counts today. Banks have graduated from daily evaluation of risk to intra-day risk evaluations.

"Risk management on a daily basis is a thing of the past because there are higher volatilities," says Sen of the marketplace today. "You can see the volatilities unfold in the marketplace when there is an event or an announcement about macro events—unemployment rate or interest rate going up or down or important geo-political events. News often causes uncertainty in the minds of investors and thus volatilities in financial markets increase. When volatility goes up during the course of a day or trading session, it has instantaneous effect on the value of financial instruments."

For market risk, the data explodes very quickly. Today, the portfolios being evaluated are quite large and include multiple financial instruments. For example, an investment bank will have a portfolio of equities, along with a portfolio of options—both calls and puts on equities. In addition, there will be foreign exchange trades, a portfolio of interest rate instruments, and interest rate derivatives. Some banks may have more complex products in their portfolios like exotic options—Bermudans, Asian options, digital options, and such.

An often used convention, according to Sen, is to calculate the mark-to-market value of the underlying financial instruments and thus calculate the risks. To show how this works, he gave us this example:

> [L]et's say that you have an investment bank that has an equity derivative in its portfolio and the value of this derivative will change in the future. That change is going to be influenced by the spot price of the underlying stock, the volatility of that stock, interest rate, and time to maturity.
>
> The convention is that every day you take the value of that derivative and you perform scenario analysis over a time horizon—the next 30 days—to determine what will be the value. Will it be $3.00 instead of $10.00 that the bank has on the books? Or will it be $13.00? In this type of scenario analysis, you create multiple scenarios and price the derivative against all the scenarios. Even for a single instrument it is possible to have hundreds of thousands of scenarios. Naturally, when you have hundreds of thousands of equity derivatives in your portfolio different equities, different maturities, and different strike prices, the problem of scenario analysis becomes very complex.

Intraday Risk Analytics, a Constant Flow of Big Data

To maintain competitive advantage, banks need to continuously evaluate their models, including the performance of the production models, and also continuously try to build new models to incorporate new variables with new and evolving macroeconomic conditions in a faster way. Banks have also moved from daily risk management to intraday risk management. Intraday risk management involves pricing the entire portfolio and calculating the risk limits of each of the counter-parties within the bank's portfolio. The problem gets very complex and computationally intensive.

Let's take an example of intraday risk evaluation of equities. The potential changes within a day include the spot price, the volatility of the underlying equity, and the risk free rate. If we do some basic scenario analysis—say 100 risk-free rate scenarios that could manifest themselves during the course of the day—that means calculating 100 scenarios for the spot price of the equity during the course of the day, 100 scenarios for volatility during the course of the day, and 100 scenarios for risk-free rate during the course of the day. For the bank to do their basic scenario analysis, it takes a million calculations for determining the value at risk for just that one instrument. And it must happen fast enough so that risk limits on the entire portfolio can be evaluated several times during the course of the day

"The only option that I can currently see," says Sen, "is to be solving these problems using a very large amount of parallelized computations and that is only possibly doable with GPUs. Using this type of high performance compute technology, we can determine value at risk for 100 million scenarios in less than ten milliseconds using just one of these GPU cards. The real power comes into play when you use multiple cards and parallelize the entire workload. That's when you can do scenario analysis across your entire portfolio in about 15 minutes."

Calculating Risk in Marketing

While risk analytics is used for risk management, banks are using risk predictive analytics for marketing as well. For example, when a bank scores its customers and prospects for credit card solicitations, it will use some risk management tools as well. In addition to determining who has a high likelihood of responding to promotional offers, the bank will want to consider the underlying risk for each of the prospects to whom the solicitations are being sent. Without taking into account risk profiles of individuals, bank promotion responses can result in customers with a higher risk profile.

"One of the challenges for retail banks," according to Sen, "is to score such large numbers of people for its marketing initiatives"

Given people's exact situation, you have to determine what are the right products to promote. Maybe somebody has a home loan but doesn't have a credit card or debit card. In addition, you also have to score your existing customers to determine the borrowers whose probabilities of not paying on their credit card, or on the mortgage, is rising. Once you know who these potential defaulters could be, you can see what you can do to mitigate risk of default. The sheer volume of the population that you have to score compounds the problem. You have to score it quickly because you have to take action promptly be it promotion or risk mitigation.

Other Industries Benefit from Financial Services' Risk Experience

Outside of financial services there are other industries that can benefit from this work, such as retail, media, and telecommunications. They are following suit to include evaluation of adverse select in their promotional offers.

While the adoption of analytics has been slower in other industries, momentum is starting to build around Big Data analytics. Marketing is an area that is clearly more mature in terms of adopting analytics in the areas of for marketing campaign management, targeted micromarketing (sending of different offers to different types of people depending on their likelihood to buy), and market basket analysis, which indicates what people buy together and more.

For example, in retail, forecasting is a key area where analytics is being applied. Customer churn analysis has been used by banks to determine who is likely to cancel their credit card or account. This is the same technique that is being used by telecommunication companies and retailers today to determine customer defection. Churn is also a factor used in determining customer lifetime value. Customer lifetime value indicates how much money a firm can make over the customer's lifetime, that is the period of association of the customer with the firm. Companies typically use the customer lifetime value to segment their customers and determine which are the customers to focus on.

The insurance industry today uses actuarial models for estimating losses. However, the emerging trend is to use Monte-Carlo simulations for estimating potential losses in insurance portfolios. These computationally complex models require a large footprint of hardware in order to handle the massive calculations. The cost of acquiring and maintaining such hardware sometimes becomes the impediment to adoption of analytics in enterprises. "With the advent of GPU technology, however, that will change," says Sen.

Another use for Big Data analytics in banks is identifying manipulative behavior or fraudulent activities in real-time so that you can mitigate or penalize the behavior immediately. For this, you have to dig through the voluminous transactions and find the patterns quickly.

"It's always good to catch the culprit but by that time—five years or five days later—a lot of honest players have been disadvantaged." And what can you do? "Well, not much. says Sen. However, Sen observes, "if you can catch it [the fraud] while it's happening, then you can focus on immediate enforcement so the manipulators can't twist the prices in the market to negatively impact the retail investor or even the institutional investor, who is a fair player. By quickly catching and correcting this market manipulative behavior you're creating a fair trading platform."

Big Data and Advances in Health Care

So far, most of our conversation around Big Data has focused on activities such as marketing, offer optimization, budget planning, business process management, supply chain management, anti-money laundering, fraud monitoring, and risk management.

Let's be honest. The average person can't relate their personal life to all of those topics. So here's a topic that has an impact on everyone's life: health care.

Big Data promises an enormous revolution in health care, with important advancements in everything from the management of chronic disease to the delivery of personalized medicine. In addition to saving and improving lives, Big Data has the potential to transform the entire health care system by replacing guesswork and intuition with objective, data-driven science (see Figure 2.4).

The health care industry is now awash in data: from biological data such as gene expression, Special Needs Plans (SNPs), proteomics, metabolomics to, more recently, next-generation gene sequence data. This exponential growth in data is further fueled by the digitization of patient-level data: stored in Electronic Health Records (EHRs) and Health Information Exchanges (HIEs), enhanced with data from imaging and test results, medical and prescription claims, and personal health devices.

—Colin Hill, CEO and President, GNS Healthcare

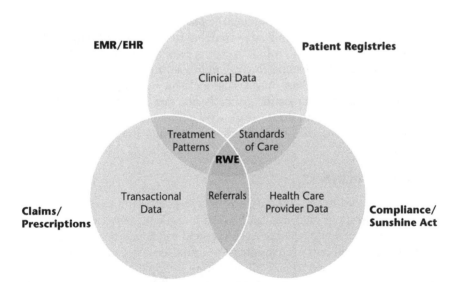

Figure 2.4   Data in the World of Health Care
Source: Jim Golden, Accenture, September 2012.

The U.S. health care system is increasingly challenged by issues of cost and access to quality care. Payers, producers, and providers are each attempting to realize improved treatment outcomes and effective benefits for patients within a disconnected health care framework. Historically, these health care ecosystem stakeholders tend to work at cross purposes with other members of the health care value chain. High levels of variability and ambiguity across these individual approaches increase costs, reduce overall effectiveness, and impede the performance of the health care system as a whole.

Recent approaches to health care reform attempt to improve access to health care by increasing government subsidies and reducing the ranks of the uninsured. One outcome of the recently passed Accountable Care Act is a revitalized focus on cost containment and the creation of quantitative proofs of economic benefit by payers, producers, and providers. A more interesting unintended consequence is an opportunity for these health care stakeholders to set aside historical differences and create a combined counterbalance to potential regulatory burdens established, without the input of the actual industry the government is setting out to regulate. This "the enemy of my enemy is my friend" mentality has created an urgent motivation for payers, producers, and, to a lesser extent, providers, to create a new health care information value chain derived from a common health care analytics approach.

The health care system is facing severe economic, effectiveness, and quality challenges. These external factors are forcing a transformation of the pharmaceutical business model.

Health care challenges are forcing the pharmaceutical business model to undergo rapid change. Our industry is moving from a traditional model built on regulatory approval and settling of claims, to one of medical evidence and proving economic effectiveness through improved analytics derived insights.

The success of this new business model will be dependent on having access to data created across the entire health care ecosystem. We believe there is an opportunity to drive competitive advantage for our LS clients by creating a robust analytics capability and harnessing integrated real-world patient level data.

"Disruptive Analytics"

The changing health care landscape is an excellent example of where data science and disruptive analytics can have an immediate beneficial impact. We believe transformation of the health care system will come through Big Data-driven decisions and improved insights. Over time, evidence of value measured in patient outcomes tied to costs derived from multiple health care Big Data assets will become the common currency across all health care sectors. Let's introduce one of the health care analytics experts we interviewed, James Golden.

James Golden is a Partner at Accenture in the pharmaceutical R&D practice. His work has included the development of systems and software for the integration and analyses of structured and unstructured health care and life science data. Jim's most recent work focuses on *evidence-based medicine* (EBM). Although the idea of EBM has been around for a while, the arrival of Big Data analytics makes it possible to transform the vision into reality, creating a transparent approach to pharmaceutical decision making based on the aggregation and analysis of health care data such as electronic medical records and insurance claims data.

Prior to joining Accenture, Golden was the chief technology officer of SAIC's Commercial Life Sciences Office, where he focused on search and intelligence analysis, including unstructured text mining, competitive intelligence, and social networks. He is a major in the U.S. Air Force Reserve and spent several years on the staff of the Air Force Test Pilot School.

According to Golden's insight, health care Big Data analytics presents an opportunity to unify the health care value chain in a way not achieved to date, a virtual form of unification with significant benefits for all stakeholders. Creating a health care analytics framework has significant value for individual stakeholders:

- For providers (physicians), there is an opportunity to build analytics systems for EBM—sifting through clinical and health outcomes data to determine the best clinical protocols that provide the best health outcome for patients and create defined standards of care.
- For producers (pharmaceutical and medical device companies), there is an opportunity to build analytics systems to enable *translational medicine* (TM)—integrating externally generated postmarketing safety, epidemiology, and health outcomes data with internally generated clinical and discovery data (sequencing, expression, biomarkers) to enable improved strategic R&D decision making across the pharmaceutical value chain.
- For payers (i.e., insurance companies), there is an opportunity to create analytics systems to enable *comparative effectiveness research* (CER) that will be used to drive reimbursement—mining large collections of claims, health care records (EMR/EHR), economic and geographic, demographic data sets to determine what treatments and therapies work best for which patients in which context and with what overall economic and outcomes benefits.

A Holistic Value Proposition

James Golden explains the theory of a holistic value proposition:

> If we believe that data is indeed a platform, then we should begin to manage it like one. It is the ability to collect, integrate, analyze and

manage this data that make health care data such as EHR/EMRs valuable. Longitudinal patient data is one source of the raw material on which evidence based insight approaches can be built to enable health care reform.

To date, there has been little attempt to "see where the data takes us" and create a holistic health care value proposition built on quantifiable evidence that clarifies business value for all stakeholders.

Because of our client relationships across the health care ecosystem, we are facilitating unique partnerships across payer, provider, pharma, and federal agencies to work on problems of health care data analytics together and create value for all health care stakeholders.

At Accenture, we are working across our life science and health care practices to identify the breadth of health care data sources that exist in order to better understand how our client's pharmaceutical and health care delivery products perform in the real world. Working with our clients, we have taken a "big data" approach to the analysis of health care data—by that we mean creating methods and platforms for the analysis of large volumes of disparate kinds of data—clinical, EMR, claims, labs, etc.—to better answer questions of outcomes, epidemiology, safety, effectiveness, and pharmacoeconomic benefit. We are leveraging big data technologies and platforms such as Hadoop, R, openhealthdata, and others to help our clients create real-world evidence-based approaches to realizing solutions for competitive effectiveness research, improve outcomes in complex populations, and to improve patient cohort segmentation and formulary decision making.

By "big data," we also mean that health care data sets are big enough to obscure underlying meaning; that traditional methods of storing, accessing, and analyzing those data are breaking down; the data itself is both structured and unstructured; and large-scale analytics are needed for critical decision making, specifically in the face of cost containment, regulatory burden, and requirements of health care reform.

Over the last decade companies such as Google, LinkedIn, eBay, and Facebook have created enormously valuable businesses that rely on the skills of new data scientists, who are linking together large data sets from disparate sources, visualizing and mining data in new ways to create novel modeling techniques, and developing new platforms for predictive analytics and decision support that impact the lives of millions of people on a daily basis. Statisticians and experts in machine learning and artificial intelligence, once relegated to academia, are becoming the new rock stars of Silicon Valley and bring multidisciplinary mathematical approaches to e-commerce and social media.

As a result, engineers and data scientists at these companies are creating the technology and expertise required to turn raw data into information assets with tangible business value. The challenge is to discover how to leverage these rapidly evolving and nonstandardized skills into an enterprise analytics group usable by health care stakeholders. IT resources within the enterprise are often older and reluctant to embrace a "hacker ethos" needed to create patient data mash-ups, new data products, and on-the-fly data mining techniques. There is very little knowledge transfer between tomorrow's Big Data scientist and today's health care CIOs.

BI Is Not Data Science

Regardless of the cultural challenges, experts like James Golden are beginning to see, across multiple industries, the desire to create quant-like groups within the organization to supply deep industry domain knowledge coupled directly with data science capabilities. These talents are relatively rare—with the exception of capital markets and energy, deep business domain knowledge and understanding of statistics, data mining, and machine learning don't often go together. Golden explains the new versus old approach:

> While soft-data science efforts have been utilized for years (think Six Sigma black belts or knowledge management teams), these skills don't really help data tell its story and transform the business through improved analytics.
>
> Traditional BI and data warehousing skills don't readily translate to predictive analytics capabilities. Renaming your EDW/BI group as quants or data scientists isn't going to cut it. Like a lawyer who draws a conclusion and then looks for supporting evidence, traditional BI is declarative and doesn't necessarily require any real domain understanding. Generating automated reports from aging data warehouses that are briefly scanned by senior management does not meet our definition of data science.

A critical point that Golden provides is that the ideal quant is as much philosophical as technical. Making data science useful to the business is about identifying the question management is really trying to answer, understanding and communicating the value of answering that question, identifying the data sources—internal and external—needed to answer the question, and then applying the right analytic method. This capability is rare in one individual, but we have found that data science teams coupled with business process experts can quickly create significant analytics value within the organization.

Pioneering New Frontiers in Medicine

The new era of data-driven health care is already producing new kinds of heroes. For example, Murali Ramanathan is co-director, Data Intensive Discovery Institute, State University of New York at Buffalo. Ramanathan uses Big Data analytics to identify the genetic variations that predispose individuals to multiple sclerosis (MS). Here's a brief description of what he does, in his own words:

> I am not a computer scientist, I'm a pharmaceutical scientist and work on the role of environmental factors, interactions between environmental factors in multiple sclerosis, which is a neurological disease. What we've got are data sets that contain thousands of genes. Typically, our data sets contain somewhere between 100,000 to 500,000 genetic variations.
>
> Our algorithms identify the interactions (between environmental factors and diseases) and they also have rapid search techniques built into them. We also want to be able to do statistical analysis. In our case, we are doing permutation analysis, which can be very, very time consuming if not properly done. With today's technology, we can get about 500,000 genetic variations in a single patient sample.

Nate Burns, a colleague of Ramanathan's at SUNY Buffalo, paints a vivid description of the challenge facing pioneers of data-intensive quantitative pharmacology:

> The data set is very large—a 1,000 by 2,000 matrix. What makes it interesting is when you try to do an interaction analysis for first and second order interactions, basically each of those 500,000 genetic locations is compared to each of all the rest of the 500,000 genetic locations for the first order; then you have to do that twice, so you've cut 500,000 to a third, for second order interactions and so on. It becomes exceedingly challenging as you move into more interactions. Basically, a second order interaction would be 500,000 squared, a third order would be 500,000 cubed, and so on.

The good news is that results from the MS study can potentially help researchers understand other autoimmune diseases (such as rheumatoid arthritis, diabetes, and lupus) and neurodegenerative diseases such as Parkinson's and Alzheimer's. "MS actually occupies a space between these two categories of diseases," says Ramanathan. "Our goal is finding the similarities and differences by looking at the data sets."

Advertising and Big Data: From Papyrus to Seeing Somebody

Let's take one of the oldest business practices, advertising, which dates back to the days when ancient Egyptians used Papyrus to make sales banners to promote their businesses. Back then it was a simple matter of promoting your business through the use of visual promotional advertising.

Now let's fast forward to an incredible scene on the streets of Madison Avenue, New York City, during the 1960s. Every present-day businessperson smirks in either jealousy or disbelief when they see the work-life of the advertising executive character from AMC's drama *Mad Men*, Donald Draper. Draper's character is partially based on Draper Daniels, the creative head of the Leo Burnett advertising agency in 1950s who created the Marlboro Man campaign. As Don said, "Just think about it deeply, then forget it . . . then an idea will jump up in your face." A bunch of executives ideating about the next big idea over Manhattan cocktails and Lucky Strike cigarettes wasn't that far from reality in those days.

With a history dating back to 1873, Foote, Cone & Belding Worldwide is one of the oldest providers of advertising and marketing services. Fairfax Cone inherited the agency from Albert Lasker, who can justifiably be called the founder of the modern advertising industry. Together with his colleagues, Emerson Foote, and Don Belding, Cone led the agency for over 30 years.

> *Advertising is what you do when you can't (afford to) go see somebody. That's all it is.*
> —Fairfax Cone, principal of Foote, Cone & Belding, 1963

Cone's quote was stated around the same time when companies were using rather primitive sales and marketing tactics to "go see someone." Salesmen were lugging Electrolux Vacuum cleaners from house to house pitching their high-end equipment and competing against manufacturers like Hoover and Oreck. The salesmen had a tough job because the only customer information they had was picking a neighborhood where they felt people could afford their product. The truth is they were not welcome at any home and were greeted with a scowl or totally ignored by people pretending to not be home. There was one key question each salesman would ask that increased their chance of being invited in, "Do you own an Electrolux?" If the answer was yes, the salesman would offer to service their equipment with a tune-up. This would result in an infrequent upsell to a new vacuum, but most of the time they were lucky if they sold a pack of new bags!

While in Great Britain, the firm launched an advertising campaign with the slogan "Nothing sucks like an Electrolux." This clever slogan was accompanied by a visual of the Leaning Tower of Pisa next to the latest series of the Electrolux vacuum. Since Electrolux is a Scandinavian-based company, most people thought this double entendre was a blunder. However, the slogan was deliberate and designed to have "stopping power," and it certainly succeeded in grabbing the audience's attention. The Electrolux vacuum brand sold very well in Great Britain for some time and people still remember the slogan. Although the campaign was rejected in the United States in the late 1960s, some think that this campaign humor would work in America today, especially during the Super Bowl.

The early advertising executives had a powerful means to reach their audiences, which was billboard, newspaper, radio, and eventually television. However, their clients were focused on the big idea because they were desperate to get their messages through these channels. As the industry matured, they demanded to learn more about their audiences, which created demand for firms such as Nielsen Media Research, which would statistically measure which television programs are watched by different segments of the population. This would help the advertisers pick the best place to place their ads (media spend). After years of refinement, clever media planning, and the inclusion of more and more data, marketers got pretty savvy at targeting their ads.

Big Data Feeds the Modern-Day Donald Draper

To get a feel for how Big Data is impacting the advertising market, we sat down with Randall Beard, who is currently the global head of Nielsen's Global Head of Advertiser Solutions. Essentially what Beard's team does is connect what people watch and what people buy to help their clients optimize advertising and media return on investment. The Nielsen experience is great, but the best part of interviewing Beard is that before Nielsen he actually worked on the client side for 25 years at companies such as the big advertising spender P&G. Needless to say, he knows his stuff.

> *What's driving all of this is not just that they're spending a lot of money but CEOs/CFOs are looking at the chief marketing officers and saying look, if we're going to spend $100 million, $500 million, a billion in advertising and media, show me the money. Show me this stuff works or we're not going to spend the money on it. There was this huge demand for accountability that's driving the need for the marketing heads to answer these questions.*
>
> —Randall Beard

Reach, Resonance, and Reaction

Beard explained that big data is now changing the way advertisers address three related needs:

1. **How much do I need to spend?** "It's basic and fundamental but it's amazing to me that we're sitting here in 2012 and advertisers still have a really hard time answering the question, How much do I need to spend next year? I know what my revenue goal is next year, and I know how much profit I need to deliver. What do I need to spend to deliver that?"

2. **How do I allocate that spend across all the marketing communication touch points?** "Answering the question, "how do I allocate my marketing communications spending across paid, owned and earned media is increasingly difficult. If you think about that question, it's getting harder and harder to answer because of the fragmentation of media, the rise of digital, and the increasing importance of social media. If I'm going to spend money in digital, how much do I allocate to banner versus rich media versus online video versus search? How about mobile, how about apps? It's further complicated by the fact that all these things work together in a complementary manner. You can't even think about them as independent things."

3. **How do I optimize my advertising effectiveness against my brand equity and ROI in real-time.** "The old paradigm was I go out and run a campaign. Maybe after the fact, I measure it . . . maybe . . . try to determine some ROI then plan for the next cycle of advertising. Basically, advertisers are saying that's not good enough. I want to know within days, or at least weeks, how my advertising is performing in the market and what levers to pull, what knobs to turn, so that I get a higher ROI."

Given these needs, advertisers need to be able to measure their advertising end to end. What does this mean?

To start with, they need to identify the people who are most volumetrically responsive to their advertising. And then answer questions such as: What do those people watch? How do I reach them? "With more and more data, and the ability to measure what people watch and buy at the household level, there is the capability to identify those people who were most volumetrically responsive to your advertising. Then you can figure out: What TV programs do those people watch? What do they do online? How do I develop my media plan against that intended audience? That's the first part of reach," explained Beard.

Now the second part of the "reach" equation is to understand if you are actually reaching your desired audience. If you think about the online world, it's a world where you can deliver 100 million impressions but you never really know for sure who your campaign was actually delivered to. If your intended audience is women aged 18 to 35, of your 100 million impressions, what percentage of impressions were actually delivered to the intended audience? What was the reach, what was the frequency, what was the delivery against the intended audience? For all the great measurement that people can do online, that hasn't been well measured historically. This is the other part of reach—delivering your ads to the right audience.

Let's now talk about resonance. If you know whom you want to reach and you're reaching them efficiently with your media spend, the next question is, are your ads breaking through? Do people know they're from your brand? Are they changing attitudes? Are they making consumers more likely to want to buy your brand? This is what I call "resonance."

Lastly, you want to measure the actual behavioral impact. If you've identified the highest potential audience, reached them efficiently with your media plan, delivered ads that broke through the clutter and increased their interest in buying your brand—did it actually result in a purchase? Did people actually buy your product or service based on exposure to your advertising? At the end of the day, advertising must drive a behavioral "reaction" or it isn't really working.

Beard explained the three guiding principles to measurement:

1. End to end measurement—reach, resonance and reaction
2. Across platforms (TV, digital, print, mobile, etc.)
3. Measured in real-time (when possible)

The Need to Act Quickly (Real-Time When Possible)

When you start executing a campaign, how do you know on a daily basis whether your advertising campaign is actually being delivered to your intended audience the way it's supposed to?

For example, in digital, ad performance will differ across websites. Certain websites are really good; certain websites are really bad. How do you optimize across sites "on the fly?" By moving money out of weak performing sites and into better performing sites.

Beard describes how real time optimization works:

> I'm one week into my new ad campaign. There's good news and bad news. The good news is that my ad is breaking thru and is highly memorable. The bad news is that consumers think my ad is for my

key competitor. I work with my agency over the weekend to edit the spot, and it goes back on air. Presto! Branding scores increase.

A week later, I see that of my three ads on air, two have high breakthrough but one is weak. I quickly take the weak performing ad off air and rotate the media spend to the higher performing ads. Breakthru scores go up!

My campaign soon moves from running only: 30's to a mix of: 15's and: 30s, a fairly typical plan. Real time data shows me that my 15s work as well as my 30s. Why spend money on 30s? I move all the weight to 15-second ads—and see scores continue to grow.

In digital, I see that brand recall increases with exposure frequency up to two exposures, and then levels off. My agency caps exposure frequency at two. I use the savings from reduced frequency to buy more sites and extend reach.

You have real-time optimization that's going on, which is data driven instead of just gut driven! The measurement tools and capabilities are enabling this and so there's a catch-up happening both in terms of advertising systems and processes, but also just the industry infrastructure to be able to actually enable all of this real-time optimization."

Measurement Can Be Tricky

Beard gave an example of the complexity of measurement. There are tools that allow you to tag digital advertising and, typically, through a panel of some kind, you can read those people who were exposed to the advertising and those who were not and measure their actual offline purchase behavior.

In doing this for a large beer client, we could see that this campaign generated (after the fact) a 20 percent sales increase among consumers exposed versus not exposed to the advertising. You (the average person) would look at that and say, wow, looks pretty good—my advertising is working.

But the sales results aren't everything. Beard elaborates on the first part of the end-to-end measurement, involving the reach:

When we looked at reach for this particular client, their intended audience was males, aged 21–29. Of their 100 million delivered impressions, only about 40 million were actually delivered to males aged 21–29. Sixty million went to someone other than their intended audience; some went to kids (not good for a beer brand); some went to people 65+. You start out by saying wow, how much better could I have done, if instead of 40% of my impressions hitting my intended audience, I had 70 or 80% of the impressions hitting them.

When you look at the 40 percent of impressions that hit the intended audience, the reach and frequency of those was something like a 10 percent reach and a 65 frequency. In other words, they only hit about 10 percent of their intended audience, but each of these people was bombarded with, on average, 65 ads! That's not quite the optimization one would hope for. There's a lot of science in advertising that shows that by maximizing reach and minimizing frequency, you get your best response. If they had been measuring all of this in real time, they could have quickly adjusted the plan to increase delivery to the intended audience, increase reach, and reduce frequency.

Content Delivery Matters Too

Let's now look at ad performance by website. The ads were on twelve websites: four were terrible; the breakthrough was terrible, branding was terrible—the ads didn't perform well in those sites. The other ones were really good. If they had measured that in flight, they could have moved spending out of the bad performing sites, into good performing sites, and further improved results.

Beard explains the importance of end-to-end measurement:

> When I think about it, it's almost like the reach times resonance equals reaction. Of course, this isn't arithmetically true, but it illustrates that while measuring the sales impact alone is great, it's not enough. You could have great sales impact and still be completely non-optimized on the reach and resonance factors that caused the reaction."

Optimization and Marketing Mixed Modeling

Marketing mixed modeling (MMM) is a tool that helps advertisers understand the impact of their advertising and other marketing activities on sales results. MMM can generally provide a solid understanding of the relative performance of advertising by medium (e.g., TV, digital, print, etc.), and in some cases can even measure sales performance by creative unit, program genre, website, and so on.

Now, we can also measure the impact on sales in social media and we do that through market mixed modeling. Market mixed modeling is a way that we can take all the different variables in the marketing mix—including paid, owned, and earned media—and use them as independent variables that we regress against sales data and trying to understand the single variable impact of all these different things.

Since these methods are quite advanced, organizations use high-end internal analytic talent and advanced analytics platforms such as SAS or point solutions such as Unica and Omniture. Alternatively, there are several boutique and large analytics providers like Mu Sigma that supply it as a software-as-a-service (SaaS).

MMM is only as good as the marketing data that is used as inputs. As the world becomes more digital, the quantity and quality of marketing data is improving, which is leading to more granular and insightful MMM analyses.

Beard's Take on the Three Big Data Vs in Advertising

Beard shared his perspective on how the three Vs (volume, velocity, and variety) have impacted advertising:

Volume

In the old days, this is not that old, not even *Mad Men* days, maybe 20 to 25 years ago, you would copy test your advertising. The agency would build a media plan demographically targeted and you'd go execute it. That was pretty much it. Maybe 6 to 12 months down the road, you'd try to use scanner data or whatever sales data you had to try to understand if there was any impact.

In today's world, there is hugely more advertising effectiveness data. On TV advertising, we can measure every ad in every TV show every day, across about 70 percent of the viewing audience in the U.S. We measure clients digital ad performance hourly—by ad, by site, by exposure, and by audience. On a daily or weekly basis, an advertiser can look at their advertising performance. The volume of information and data that is available to the advertiser has gone up exponentially versus what it was 20 years ago.

Velocity

There are already companies that will automate and optimize your advertising on the web without any human intervention at all based on click-thru. It's now beginning to happen on metrics like break-through, branding, purchase intent, and things like that. This is sometimes called programmatic buying. Literally, you'll have systems in place that will be measuring the impact of the advertising across websites or different placements within websites, figuring out where the advertising is performing best. It will be automated optimization and reallocation happening in real-time. The volume and the velocity of data, the pace at which you can get the data, make decisions and do things about it is dramatically increased.

Variety

Before, you really didn't have a lot of data about how your advertising was performing in market. You have a lot more data and it's a lot more granular. You can look at your brand's overall advertising performance in the market. But you can also decompose it to how much of a performance is due to the creative quality, due to the media weight, how much is due to the program that the ads sit in. How much is due to placement: time of day, time of year, pod position, how much is due to cross-platform exposure, how much is due to competitive activity. Then you have the ability to optimize on most of those things—in real time. And now you can also measure earned (social) and owned media. Those are all things that weren't even being measured before."

Using Consumer Products as a Doorway

As an experienced business executive, what would you say if you were asked by your boss to consider entering into the mobile phone or PC/tablet business, which the company has never tried to do before? Chances are your answer would be no way! First of all, the hardware business has a lot of manufacturing overhead, which means margins are razor thin. Second, the space is overcrowded with mature players and other low-cost providers. Last, there are dozens of consumer hardware business case nightmares such as Research in Motion (RIM), the maker of Blackberry. "Over the last year, RIM's share price has plunged 75 percent. The company once commanded more than half of the American smartphone market. Today it has 10 percent."[5] Hopefully, RIM will have the fortune to turn things around for their employees and shareholders, but we can't help but to remind ourselves of powerhouses like Gateway computing that disappeared in 2007. And companies with deep pockets and resources such as Hewlett Packard (HP) that failed to enter the tablet market, while Apple is selling iPads in its sleep.

It made a lot of sense that Apple entered into the mobile and tablet market because, after all, it is a software and hardware player that made the iPod, which crushed giants like Sony in the MP3 market. That one was a hard pill to swallow for Sony when their Walkman was all the rage through the cassette and CD years. For Apple, the market was not just about selling hardware or music on iTunes. It gave them a chance to get as close to a consumer as anyone can possibly get. This close interaction also generated a lot of data that help them expand and capture new customers. Again it's all about the data, analytics, and putting it into action.

Google gives away product that other companies, such as Microsoft, license for the same the reason. It also began playing in the mobile hardware space through the development of the Android platform and the acquisition of Motorola. It's all about gathering consumer data and monetizing the data. Do you use Google? Check out your Google Dashboard. You can see every search you did, e-mails you sent, IM messages, web-based phone calls, documents you viewed, and so on. How powerful is that for marketers? We'd say that would be similar to meeting somebody!

Who would have thought that an online retailer, Amazon, would create hardware with their Kindle Fire and that Barnes and Noble would release the Nook? Imagine that both companies know every move you make, what you download, what you search for, and now they can study your behaviors to present new products that they believe will appeal to you. It all comes down to the race for the connection with consumers and more importantly taking action on the derived data to win the marathon.

Notes

1. Avinash Kaushik, *Web Analytics 2.0: The Art of Online Accountability and Science of Customer Centricity* (Indianapolis, Indiana: Sybex, 2010).
2. Javelin Strategy & Research, "8TH Annual Card Issuers' Safety Scorecard: Proliferation of Alerts Lead to Quicker Detection Time and Lower Fraud Costs," June 2012, www .javelinstrategy.com/brochure/254.
3. Javelin Strategy & Research, "2012 Identity Fraud Report: Social Media and Mobile Forming the New Fraud Frontier," February 2012, https://www.javelinstrategy.com/news/1314/92/ Identity-Fraud-Rose-13-Percent-in-2011-According-to-New-Javelin-Strategy-Research-Report/d,pressRoomDetail.
4. Vendor content published by Experian on BankersOnline.com, January 5, 2009.
5. Sam Grobart and Ian Austen, "The BlackBerry, Trying to Avoid the Hall of Fallen Giants," *New York Times*, January 28, 2012.

CHAPTER 3

Big Data Technology

echnology is radically changing the way data is produced, processed, analyzed, and consumed. On one hand, technology helps evolve new and more effective data sources. On the other, as more and more data gets captured, technology steps in to help process this data quickly, efficiently, and visualize it to drive informed decisions. Now, more than any other time in the short history of analytics, technology plays an increasingly pivotal role in the entire process of how we gather and use data.

The Elephant in the Room: Hadoop's Parallel World

There are many Big Data technologies that have been making an impact on the new technology stacks for handling Big Data, but Apache Hadoop is one technology that has been the darling of Big Data talk. Hadoop is an open-source platform for storage and processing of diverse data types that enables data-driven enterprises to rapidly derive the complete value from all their data.

We spoke with Amr Awadallah, the cofounder and chief technology officer (CTO) of Cloudera, a leading provider of Apache Hadoop-based software and services, since it was formed in October 2008. He explained the history and overview of Hadoop to us:

> The original creators of Hadoop are Doug Cutting (used to be at Yahoo! now at Cloudera) and Mike Cafarella (now teaching at the University of Michigan in Ann Arbor). Doug and Mike were building a project called "Nutch" with the goal of creating a large Web index. They saw the MapReduce and GFS papers from Google, which were obviously super relevant to the problem Nutch was trying to solve. They integrated the concepts from MapReduce and GFS into Nutch; then later these two components were pulled out to form the genesis of the Hadoop project.
>
> The name "Hadoop" itself comes from Doug's son, he just made the word up for a yellow plush elephant toy that he has. Yahoo! hired Doug and invested significant resources into growing the Hadoop

project, initially to store and index the Web for the purpose of Yahoo! Search. That said, the technology quickly mushroomed throughout the whole company as it proved to be a big hammer that can solve many problems.

In 2008, recognizing the huge potential of Hadoop to transform data management across multiple industries, Amr left Yahoo! to co-found Cloudera with Mike Olson and Jeff Hammerbacher. Doug Cutting followed in 2009.

Moving beyond rigid legacy frameworks, Hadoop gives organizations the flexibility to ask questions across their structured and unstructured data that were previously impossible to ask or solve:

- The scale and variety of data have permanently overwhelmed the ability to cost-effectively extract value using traditional platforms.
- The scalability and elasticity of free, open-source Hadoop running on standard hardware allow organizations to hold onto more data than ever before, at a transformationally lower TCO than proprietary solutions and thereby take advantage of *all* their data to increase operational efficiency and gain a competitive edge. At one-tenth the cost of traditional solutions, Hadoop excels at supporting complex analyses— including detailed, special-purpose computation—across large collections of data.
- Hadoop handles a variety of workloads, including search, log processing, recommendation systems, data warehousing, and video/image analysis. Today's explosion of data types and volumes means that Big Data equals big opportunities and Apache Hadoop empowers organizations to work on the most modern scale-out architectures using a clean-sheet design data framework, without vendor lock-in.
- Apache Hadoop is an open-source project administered by the Apache Software Foundation. The software was originally developed by the world's largest Internet companies to capture and analyze the data that they generate. Unlike traditional, structured platforms, Hadoop is able to store any kind of data in its native format and to perform a wide variety of analyses and transformations on that data. Hadoop stores terabytes, and even petabytes, of data inexpensively. It is robust and reliable and handles hardware and system failures automatically, without losing data or interrupting data analyses.
- Hadoop runs on clusters of commodity servers and each of those servers has local CPUs and disk storage that can be leveraged by the system.

The two critical components of Hadoop are:

1. **The Hadoop Distributed File System (HDFS).** HDFS is the storage system for a Hadoop cluster. When data lands in the cluster, HDFS breaks it into pieces and distributes those pieces among the different servers participating in the cluster. Each server stores just a small fragment of the complete data set, and each piece of data is replicated on more than one server.

2. **MapReduce.** Because Hadoop stores the entire dataset in small pieces across a collection of servers, analytical jobs can be distributed, in parallel, to each of the servers storing part of the data. Each server evaluates the question against its local fragment simultaneously and reports its results back for collation into a comprehensive answer. MapReduce is the agent that distributes the work and collects the results.

Both HDFS and MapReduce are designed to continue to work in the face of system failures. HDFS continually monitors the data stored on the cluster. If a server becomes unavailable, a disk drive fails, or data is damaged, whether due to hardware or software problems, HDFS automatically restores the data from one of the known good replicas stored elsewhere on the cluster. Likewise, when an analysis job is running, MapReduce monitors progress of each of the servers participating in the job. If one of them is slow in returning an answer or fails before completing its work, MapReduce automatically starts another instance of that task on another server that has a copy of the data. Because of the way that HDFS and MapReduce work, Hadoop provides scalable, reliable, and fault-tolerant services for data storage and analysis at very low cost.

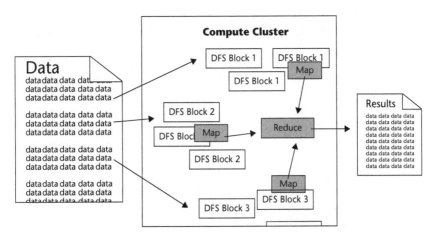

Source: Apache Software Foundation.

Old vs. New Approaches

We interviewed data guru Abhishek Mehta to get his perceptions of the differences between the "old" and "new" types of big data analytics. Mehta is a former Bank of America executive and MIT Media Lab executive-in-residence. He recently launched Tresata, a company that is developing the first Hadoop-powered Big Data analytics platform focused on financial industry data. Here is a summary of what Mehta told us:

> The old way is a data and analytics technology stack with different layers "cross-communicating data" and working on "scale-up" expensive hardware. The new way is a data and analytics platform that does all the data processing and analytics in one "layer," without moving data back and forth on cheap but scalable ("scale out") commodity hardware. This is a mega shift and a complete game changer!
>
> The new approach is based on two foundational concepts. Number one, data needs to be stored in a system in which the hardware is infinitely scalable. In other words, you cannot allow hardware (storage and network) to become the bottleneck. Number two, data must be processed, and converted into usable business intelligence where it sits. Put simply, you must move the code to the data and not the other way around. That is a fundamental departure and the primary difference between the old way and the new way. In the old ways, you had the multiple tiers of the stack and in the new way we have what is essentially a horizontal platform for data. The data sits in one place, you never move it around. That's the "secret" to big data analytics.
>
> And here's another important point to remember: The technology stack has changed. New proprietary technologies and open-source inventions enable different approaches that make it easier and more affordable to store, manage, and analyze data. So it's not a coincidence that all of this change is occurring right now.
>
> Hardware and storage are more affordable than ever before, and continuing to get cheaper [thanks to Dr. Moore], which allows for increasingly larger and more ambitious massively parallel architectures. As the sheer quantity and complexity of data increases, our ability to handle complex and unstructured data is also rising.
>
> Today we can run the algorithm, look at the results, extract the results, and feed the business process—automatically and at massive scale, using all of the data available.

We continue our conversation with Mehta later in the book. For the moment, let's boil his observations down to three main points:

1. The technology stack has changed. New proprietary technologies and open-source inventions enable different approaches that make it easier and more affordable to store, manage, and analyze data.
2. Hardware and storage is affordable and continuing to get cheaper to enable massive parallel processing.
3. The variety of data is on the rise and the ability to handle unstructured data is on the rise.

Data Discovery: Work the Way People's Minds Work

There is a lot of buzz in the industry about *data discovery*, the term used to describe the new wave of business intelligence that enables users to explore data, make discoveries, and uncover insights in a dynamic and intuitive way versus predefined queries and preconfigured drill-down dashboards. This approach has resonated with many business users who are looking for the freedom and flexibility to view Big Data. In fact, there are two software companies that stand out in the crowd by growing their businesses at unprecedented rates in this space: Tableau Software and QlikTech International.

Both companies' approach to the market is much different than the traditional BI software vendor. They grew through a sales model that many refer to as "land and expand." It basically works by getting intuitive software in the hands of some business users to get in the door and grow upward. In the past, BI players typically went for the big IT sale to be the preferred tool for IT to build reports for the business users to then come and use.

In order to succeed at the BI game of the "land and expand model," you need a product that is easy to use with lots of sexy output. One of the most interesting facts about Tableau Software is that the company's chief scientist and cofounder, Pat Hanrahan, is not a BI software veteran—he's actually an Academy Award–winning professor and founding member of Pixar! He invented the technology that helped change the world of animated film. Harahan's invention made it possible to bring some of the world's most beloved characters to the big screen, such as Buzz Lightyear and Woody the cowboy. Imagine the new creative lens that Pat brought to the BI software market!

When you have a product that is "easy to use," it also means that you have what Harahan and his colleagues call the "self-service approach," versus the traditional approach with heavy reliance on IT. Pat, co-founder Chris Stolte, and colleague Dan Jewett stated in a recent whitepaper:

> Analytics and reporting are produced by the people using the results. IT provides the infrastructure, but business people create their own reports and dashboards.
>
> The most important characteristic of rapid-fire BI is that business users, not specialized developers, drive the applications. The result is that everyone wins. The IT team can stop the backlog of change requests and instead spend time on strategic IT issues. Users can serve themselves data and reports when needed.
>
> The traditional practice of trying to anticipate the analytic needs of each employee is impossible—can an IT department really read the minds of business users? Business users are more productive when answering questions with their own tools.[1]

There is a simple example of powerful visualization that the Tableau team is referring to. A company uses an interactive dashboard to track the critical metrics driving their business. Every day, the CEO and other executives are plugged in real-time to see how their markets are performing in terms of sales and profit, what the service quality scores look like against advertising investments, and how products are performing in terms of revenue and profit. Interactivity is key: a click on any filter lets the executive look into specific markets or products. She can click on any data point in any one view to show the related data in the other views. Hovering over a data point lets her winnow into any unusual pattern or outlier by showing details on demand. Or she can click through the underlying information in a split-second.

We also spoke with Qliktech's CTO, Anthony Deighton, to get his view on the world of data discovery. Deighton is an ex-Seibel executive who has been with Qliktech since 2005. He is responsible for guiding product strategy and leads all aspects of the company's R&D efforts for its product suite, named QlikView. Deighton started off the interview with a very simple message: "Business intelligence needs to work the way people's minds work. Users need to navigate and interact with data any way they want to—asking and answering questions on their own and in big groups or teams."

One capability that we have all become accustomed to is search, what many people refer to as "Googling." This is a prime example of the way people's minds work. Qliktech has designed a way for users to leverage direct—and indirect—search. With QlikView search, users type relevant words or phrases in any order and get instant, associative results. With a global search bar, users can search across the entire data set. With search boxes on individual list boxes, users can confine the search to just that field. Users can conduct both direct and indirect searches. For example, if a user wanted to identify a sales rep but couldn't remember the sales rep's name—just details about the person, such as that he sells fish to customers in the Nordic region—the user could search on the sales rep list box for "Nordic" and "fish" to narrow the search results to just the people who meet those criteria.

Open-Source Technology for Big Data Analytics

Open-source software is computer software that is available in source code form under an open-source license that permits users to study, change, and improve and at times also to distribute the software. The open-source name came out of a 1998 meeting in Palo Alto in reaction to Netscape's announcement of a source code release for Navigator (as Mozilla).

Although the source code is released, there are still governing bodies and agreements in place. The most prominent and popular example is the GNU General Public License (GPL), which "allows free distribution under the condition that further developments and applications are put under the same license." This ensures that the products keep improving over time for the greater population of users.

Some other open-source projects are managed and supported by commercial companies, such as Cloudera, that provide extra capabilities, training, and professional services that support open-source projects such as Hadoop. This is similar to what Red Hat has done for the open-source project Linux.

"One of the key attributes of the open-source analytics stack is that it's not constrained by someone else's predetermined ideas or vision," says David Champagne, chief technology officer at Revolution Analytics, a provider of advanced analytics. "The open-source stack doesn't put you into a straitjacket. You can make it into what you want and what you need. If you come up with an idea, you can put it to work immediately. That's the advantage of the open-source stack—flexibility, extensibility, and lower cost."

"One of the great benefits of open source lies in the flexibility of the adoption model: you download and deploy it when you need it," said Yves de Montcheuil, vice president of marketing at Talend, a provider of open-source data integration solutions. "You don't need to prove to a vendor that you have a million dollars in your budget. With open source, you can try it and adopt it at your own pace."

David Smith of Revolution Analytics has written many blogs and papers about the new open-source analytics stack. Smith is vice president of marketing at Revolution Analytics in Palo Alto. He observes that the pace of software development has accelerated dramatically because of open-source software. He follows this observation by describing how this phenomenon is setting the stage for a new "golden age" of software development:

> In the past, the pace of software development was moderated by a relatively small set of proprietary software vendors. But there are clear signs that the old software development model is crumbling, and that a new model is replacing it.

The old model's end state was a monolithic stack of proprietary tools and systems that could not be swapped out, modified, or upgraded without the original vendor's support. This model was largely unchallenged for decades. The status quo rested on several assumptions, including:

1. The amounts of data generated would be manageable
2. Programming resources would remain scarce
3. Faster data processing would require bigger, more expensive hardware

Many of those underlying assumptions have now disappeared, David writes:

The sudden increase in demand for software capable of handling significantly larger data sets, coupled with the existence of a worldwide community of open-source programmers, has upended the status quo.

The traditional analytics stack is among the first "victims" of this revolution. David explains how it has changed the game of enterprise software:

The old model was top-down, slow, inflexible and expensive. The new software development model is bottom-up, fast, flexible, and considerably less costly.

A traditional proprietary stack is defined and controlled by a single vendor, or by a small group of vendors. It reflects the old command-and-control mentality of the traditional corporate world and the old economic order.

David then makes the case for an open-source analytics stack. For David, who is a leading proponent of open-source analytics, it's a logical leap:

An open-source stack is defined by its community of users and contributors. No one "controls" an open-source stack, and no one can predict exactly how it will evolve. The open-source stack reflects the new realities of the networked global economy, which is increasingly dependent on big data.

It's certainly fair to argue whether the new analytics stack should be open, proprietary, or a blend of the two. From our perspective, it seems unlikely that large companies will abandon their investments in existing proprietary technologies overnight.

Our hunch is that open-source and proprietary solutions will coexist for a long time, and for many good reasons. In fact, most proprietary vendors have been designing their solutions to plug and play with technology such as Hadoop. For example, Teradata Aster designed SQL-H, which is a seamless way to execute SQL and SQL-MapReduce on Apache Hadoop data.

Tasso Argyros is copresident of Teradata Aster, leading the Aster Center of Innovation. In a recent blog, Argyros explained the significance of his firm's integration with open-source Hadoop:

> This is a significant step forward from what was state-of-the-art until yesterday. This means that [in the past] getting data from Hadoop to a database required a Hadoop expert in the middle to do the data cleansing and the data type translation. If the data was not 100% clean (which is the case in most circumstances) a developer was needed to get it to a consistent, proper form. Besides wasting the valuable time of that expert, this process meant that business analysts couldn't directly access and analyze data in Hadoop clusters. SQL-H, an industry-first, solves all those problems.[2]

The Cloud and Big Data

It is important to remember that for all kinds of reasons—technical, political, social, regulatory, and cultural—cloud computing has not been a successful business model that has been widely adopted for enterprises to store their Big Data assets. However, there are many who believe that some obvious industry verticals will soon realize that there is a huge ROI opportunity if they do embrace the cloud.

> *There will be Big Data platforms that companies will build, especially for the core operational systems of the world. Where we continue to have an explosive amount of data come in and because the data is so proprietary that building out an infrastructure in-house seems logical. I actually think it's going to go to the cloud, it's just a matter of time! It's not value add enough to collect, process and store data.*
>
> —Avinash Kaushik, Google's digital marketing evangelist

Abhishek Mehta is one of those individuals who believes that cloud models are inevitable for every industry and it's just a matter of when an industry will shift to the cloud model. He explains that his clients are saying, "I don't have unlimited capital to invest in infrastructure. My data is exploding—both structured and unstructured. The models that I use to price products or manage risks are broken. I'm under immense pressure to streamline my operations and reduce headcount. How am I going to solve these problems?"

Market economics are demanding that capital-intensive infrastructure costs disappear and business challenges are forcing clients to consider newer models. At the crossroads of high capital costs and rapidly changing business needs is a sea change that is driving the need for a new, compelling value proposition that is being manifested in a cloud-deployment model.

With a cloud model, you pay on a subscription basis with no upfront capital expense. You don't incur the typical 30 percent maintenance fees—and all the updates on the platform are automatically available. The traditional cost of value chains is being completely disintermediated by platforms—massively scalable platforms where the marginal cost to deliver an incremental product or service is zero.

The ability to build massively scalable platforms—platforms where you have the option to keep adding new products and services for zero additional cost—is giving rise to business models that weren't possible before. Mehta calls it "the next industrial revolution, where the raw material is data and data factories replace manufacturing factories." He pointed out a few guiding principles that his firm stands by:

1. **Stop saying "cloud."** It's not about the fact that it is virtual, but the true value lies in delivering software, data, and/or analytics in an "as a service" model. Whether that is in a private hosted model or a publicly shared one does not matter. The delivery, pricing, and consumption model matters.
2. **Acknowledge the business issues.** There is no point to make light of matters around information privacy, security, access, and delivery. These issues are real, more often than not heavily regulated by multiple government agencies, and unless dealt with in a solution, will kill any platform sell.
3. **Fix some core technical gaps.** Everything from the ability to run analytics at scale in a virtual environment to ensuring information processing and analytics authenticity are issues that need solutions and have to be fixed.

Predictive Analytics Moves into the Limelight

To master analytics, enterprises will move from being in reactive positions (business intelligence) to forward leaning positions (predictive analytics).

Using all the data available—traditional internal data sources combined with new rich external data sources—will make the predictions more accurate and meaningful.

Because the analytics are contextual, enterprises can build confidence in the analytics and the trust will result in using analytic insights to trigger business events. By automatically triggering events, the friction in business will be greatly reduced. Algorithmic trading and supply chain optimization are just two typical examples where predictive analytics have greatly reduced the friction in business. Look for predictive analytics to proliferate in every facet of our lives, both personal and business. Here are some leading trends that are making their way to the forefront of businesses today:

- Recommendation engines similar to those used in Netflix and Amazon that use past purchases and buying behavior to recommend new purchases.
- Risk engines for a wide variety of business areas, including market and credit risk, catastrophic risk, and portfolio risk.
- Innovation engines for new product innovation, drug discovery, and consumer and fashion trends to predict potential new product formulations and discoveries.
- Customer insight engines that integrate a wide variety of customer-related info, including sentiment, behavior, and even emotions. Customer insight engines will be the backbone in online and set-top box advertisement targeting, customer loyalty programs to maximize customer lifetime value, optimizing marketing campaigns for revenue lift, and targeting individuals or companies at the right time to maximize their spend.
- Optimization engines that optimize complex interrelated operations and decisions that are too overwhelming for people to systematically handle at scales, such as when, where, and how to seek natural resources to maximize output while reducing operational costs— or what potential competitive strategies should be used in a global business that takes into account the various political, economic, and competitive pressures along with both internal and external operational capabilities.

Today we are at the tip of the iceberg in terms of applying predictive analytics to real-world problems. With predictive analytics you can realize the uncontested market space [competitive free] that Kim and Mauborgne described in *Blue Ocean Strategy*.[3]

Software as a Service BI

The software industry has seen some successful companies excel in the game of *software as a service* (SaaS) industry, such as salesforce.com. The basic principal is to make it easy for companies to gain access to solutions without the headache of building and maintaining their own onsite implementation. When you add up the costs of the people and technology, SaaS is far less expensive too. The solutions are typically sold by vendors on a subscription or pay-as-you-go basis instead of the more traditional software licensing model with annual maintenance fees.

According to a recent article in *TechTarget*, "SaaS BI can be a good choice when there's little or no budget money available for buying BI software and related hardware. Because there aren't any upfront purchase costs or additional staffing requirements needed to manage the BI system, total cost of ownership (TCO) may be lower than it is with on-premise software—although overall SaaS BI costs will depend on the amount of usage the tools get."[4]

Another common buying factor for SaaS is the immediate access to talent, especially in the world of information management, business intelligence (BI), and predictive analytics. More than a decade ago, analytics legend John Brocklebank of SAS (not to be confused with SaaS) created a thriving analytics on-demand center that allows companies to gain access to Ph.D.-level statisticians who deliver sophisticated output within a simple BI portal. This is now one of SAS's fastest growing lines of business, which is logical given the shortage in predictive analytics talent.

In the world of web analytics, there was another significant SaaS BI invention named Omniture (now owned by Adobe). Omniture's success was fueled by their ability to handle Big Data in the form of weblog data. We spoke with Josh James, the creator of Omniture and now the founder and CEO of Domo, a SaaS BI provider. Our first question for James was why his business was so successful:

> In addition to the Omniture people, several other reasons stand out to me. They include:
>
> - **Scaling the SaaS delivery model.** We built Omniture from the ground up to be SaaS and we understood the math better than the competition. We invented a concept called the Magic Number. The Magic Number helps you look at your SaaS business and helps you understand the value you are creating when standard GAAP accounting numbers would lead you to believe the opposite.
> - **Killer sales organization.** Once we had a few well-known customers like HP, eBay, and Gannett, we stepped on the pedal from a

competitive standpoint and really went to battle against the other sales organizations and we won. We focused the whole company on sales.

- **A focus on customer success.** We had 98 percent retention rate. Customer happiness and success were always first because in a SaaS business, unlike traditional enterprise software, it's too easy for customers to leave if they are not happy. James explained the three market reasons why he started Domo, knowing we had to fix three problems in traditional BI. Here is a summary in his own words:

  1. **Relieving the IT choke point.** Removing the friction for BI to become useful and enabling IT to be more strategic by enabling self-service BI.

  2. **Transforming BI from cost center to a revenue generator.** Addresses a very common frustration that I've experienced as a CEO and that other CEOs have shared with me . . . now that we've invested in capturing all this data—how do we benefit from it?

  3. **The user experience.** Is where we are putting all our marbles. Today's BI is not designed for the end user. It's not intuitive, it's not accessible, it's not real time, and it doesn't meet the expectations of today's consumers of technology, who expect a much more connected experience than enterprise software delivers. We'll deliver an experience with BI that redefines BI and is unlike anything seen to date.

Although this model makes a lot of sense, we can't help but remind ourselves that there are two sides to every decision. Tech Target pointed out: "With SaaS BI the analysis tools may not have all the features that on-premise software products do—which may make them less complex and difficult to use, but also less functional. Sending corporate data beyond the firewall also raises red flags for some IT managers. To try to assuage those concerns, some vendors have created private analytic clouds that run inside a customer's firewall."[5]

Mobile Business Intelligence Is Going Mainstream

Analytics on mobile devices is what some refer to as putting BI in your pocket. Mobile drives straight to the heart of simplicity and ease of use that has been a major barrier to BI adoption since day one. Mobile devices are a great leveling field where making complicated actions easy is the name of the game. For example, a young child can use an iPad but not a laptop. As a result, this will drive broad-based adoption as much for the ease of use as for the mobility these devices offer. This will have an immense impact on the business intelligence sector.

We interviewed Dan Kerzner, SVP Mobile at MicroStrategy, a leading provider of business intelligence software. He has been in the BI space for quite a while. People have been talking about mobile BI for quite some time, especially since the 1999 release of the good-old BlackBerry. However, it seems as though we have finally hit an inflection point. Kerzner explains his view on this topic:

> We have been working on Mobile BI for a while but the iPad was the inflection point where I think it started to become mainstream. I have seen customers over the past decade who focused on the mobile space generally and mobile applications in particular. One client in particular told me that he felt like he was pushing a boulder up a hill until he introduced mobility to enhance productivity. Once the new smart phones and tablets arrived, his phone was ringing off the hook and he was trying to figure out which project to say yes to, because he couldn't say yes to everyone who suddenly wanted mobile analytics in the enterprise.

That experience of folks who have been trying to use mobility for a long time to drive productivity and having really only pockets of success and then suddenly flipping over and becoming very pervasive is starting to be well understood now. In terms of why that's the case, Dan's perspective on that is that with the advent of touch-driven devices, you get a set of phones that are really much more about software than they are about being a phone:

> You turn off the iPhone and it's kind of a brick, nothing to it. It doesn't look like a phone. But you turn it on and the animating experience of it is the screen and the software that flows through that screen and the usability you get from having that touch-driven device. What's happened is suddenly you get a world where you actually have a form factor which lends itself to the power and flexibility, creativity, and innovation that comes with software development. That hadn't really been the case before. You sort of had it with some of the Palm organizer devices that were out there and you started to have it in a light-touch way with the early Blackberries. But it was always still your phone first, your messaging, you weren't fundamentally software driven. I think the combination of multi-touch and having a software oriented device is what has unlocked the potential of these devices to really bring mobile analytics and intelligence to a much wider audience in a productive way.

Ease of Mobile Application Deployment

Another inflection point for the industry is the development and deployment of mobile applications. In the past, that was controlled by the relationship with the carrier. It used to be that if you wanted to push out a mobile application, the only way you could get that application on the phone for the most part was to go through the carriers. That meant there were development environments that were sometimes very proprietary or you had to develop one set of applications for one carrier and another set of applications for a different one, maybe a third for the RIM BlackBerry environment. It didn't lend itself to very fast detonation because there was a real channel control now. Kerzner elaborated:

> One of the things that's happened recently is that with the advent of these app stores and the maturing of the browsers on the devices into something much more powerful, now as a software provider, you can go directly to the end user. I can go to a corporation and say I'm going to roll out a powerful global reporting application that's also going to do deal approvals and it's going to totally change a whole business process. I think something that was previously locked in a desk will now give people insights into the purchasing patterns, as well as the ability to take that action. I can roll out that whole application— I never have to talk to anybody but that customer because the devices that everybody's lugging around are really little computers and of course you can put any software you want on a little computer and that really wasn't the case historically in the mobile space.

Three elements that have impacted the viability of mobile BI:

1. Location—the GPS component and location . . . know where you are in time as well as the movement.
2. It's not just about pushing data; you can transact with your smart phone based on information you get.
3. Multimedia functionality allows the visualization pieces to really come into play.

Three challenges with mobile BI include:

1. Managing standards for rolling out these devices.
2. Managing security (always a big challenge).
3. Managing "bring your own device," where you have devices both owned by the company and devices owned by the individual, both contributing to productivity.

Crowdsourcing Analytics

In October 2006, Netflix, an online DVD rental business, announced a contest to create a new predictive model for recommending movies based on past user ratings. The grand prize was $1,000,000! While this may seem like a PR gimmick, it wasn't. Netflix already had an algorithm to solve the problem but thought there was an opportunity to realize additional model "lift," which would translate to huge top-line revenue. Netflix was an innovator in a space now being termed *crowdsourcing*. Crowdsourcing is a recognition that you can't possibly always have the best and brightest internal people to solve all your big problems. By creating an open, competitive environment with clear rules and goals, Netflix realized their objective and, yes, they did create a lot of buzz about their organization in the process.

Crowdsourcing is a great way to capitalize on the resources that can build algorithms and predictive models. Let's face it, you can't "grow" a Ph.D. (or big brain) overnight. It takes years of learning and experience to get the knowledge to create algorithms and predictive models. So crowd sourcing is a way to capitalize on the limited resources that are available in the marketplace.

It's often been said that competition brings out the best in us. We are all attracted to contests; our passion for competing seems hardwired into our souls. Apparently, even predictive modelers find the siren song of competition irresistible.

That's what a small Australian firm, Kaggle, has discovered—when given the chance, data scientists love to duke it out, just like everyone else. Kaggle describes itself as "an innovative solution for statistical/analytics outsourcing." That's a very formal way of saying that Kaggle manages competitions among the world's best data scientists.

Here's how it works: Corporations, governments, and research laboratories are confronted with complex statistical challenges. They describe the problems to Kaggle and provide data sets. Kaggle converts the problems and the data into contests that are posted on its web site. The contests feature cash prizes ranging in value from $100 to $3 million. Kaggle's clients range in size from tiny start-ups to multinational corporations such as Ford Motor Company and government agencies such as NASA.

According to Anthony Goldbloom, Kaggle's founder and CEO, "The idea is that someone comes to us with a problem, we put it up on our website, and then people from all over the world can compete to see who can produce the best solution."

In essence, Kaggle has developed a remarkably effective global platform for crowdsourcing thorny analytic problems. What's especially attractive about

Kaggle's approach is that it is truly a win-win scenario—contestants get access to real-world data (that has been carefully "anonymized" to eliminate privacy concerns) and prize sponsors reap the benefits of the contestants' creativity.

Crowdsourcing is a disruptive business model whose roots are in technology but is extending beyond technology to other areas. There are various types of crowdsourcing, such as crowd voting, crowd purchasing, wisdom of crowds, crowd funding, and contests. Take for example:

- 99designs.com/, which does crowdsourcing of graphic design
- agentanything.com/, which posts "missions" where agents vie for to run errands
- 33needs.com/, which allows people to contribute to charitable programs that make a social impact

Inter- and Trans-Firewall Analytics

Over the last 100 years, supply chains have evolved to connect multiple companies and enable them to collaborate to create enormous value to the end consumer via concepts such as CPFR, VMI, and so on. Decision science is witnessing a similar trend as enterprises are beginning to collaborate on insights across the value chain. For instance, in the health care industry, rich consumer insights can be generated by collaborating on data and insights from the health insurance provider, pharmacy delivering the drugs, and the drug manufacturer. In-fact, this is not necessarily limited to companies within the traditional demand-supply value chain. For example, there are instances where a retailer and a social media company can come together to share insights on consumer behavior that will benefit both players. Some of the more progressive companies are taking this a step further and working on leveraging the large volumes of data outside the firewall such as social data, location data, and so forth. In other words, it will be not very long before internal data and insights from within the firewall is no longer a differentiator. We see this trend as the move from intra- to inter- and trans-firewall analytics. Yesterday companies were doing functional silo-based analytics. Today they are doing intra-firewall analytics with data within the firewall. Tomorrow they will be collaborating on insights with other companies to do inter-firewall analytics as well as leveraging the public domain spaces to do trans-firewall analytics (see Figure 3.1).

As Figure 3.2 depicts, setting up inter-firewall and trans-firewall analytics can add significant value. However it does present some challenges. First, as one moves outside the firewall, the information-to-noise ratio increases, putting additional requirements on analytical methods and technology requirements. Further, organizations are often limited by a fear of collaboration

Organizations will need to complement just intra-firewall insights with inter- and trans-firewall analytics

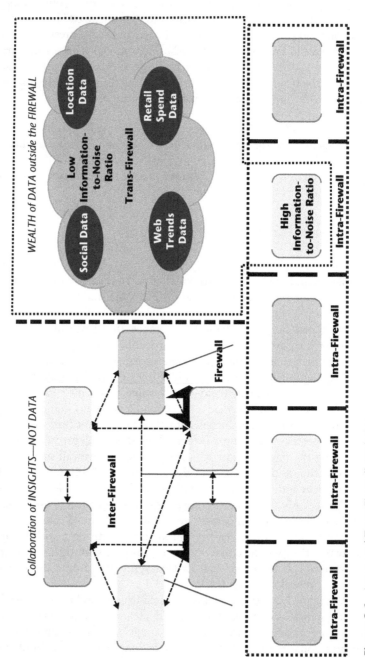

Figure 3.1 Inter- and Trans-Firewall Analytics
Source: Mu Sigma and author Ambiga is a cofounder.

Disruptive value and efficiencies can be extracted by cooperating and exploring outside the boundaries of the firewall

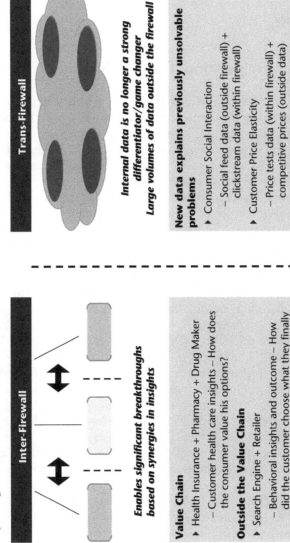

Inter-Firewall

Trans-Firewall

Internal data is no longer a strong differentiator/game changer
Large volumes of data outside the firewall

Enables significant breakthroughs based on synergies in insights

New data explains previously unsolvable problems

▶ Consumer Social Interaction
  – Social feed data (outside firewall) + clickstream data (within firewall)
▶ Customer Price Elasticity
  – Price tests data (within firewall) + competitive prices (outside data)
  – What is the sensitivity to price changes in the presence of competitor pricing?

Value Chain

▶ Health Insurance + Pharmacy + Drug Maker
  – Customer health care insights – How does the consumer value his options?

Outside the Value Chain

▶ Search Engine + Retailer
  – Behavioral insights and outcome – How did the customer choose what they finally bought?

Figure 3.2 Value Chain for Inter-Firewall and Trans-Firewall Analytics
Source: Mu Sigma.

79

and an overreliance on proprietary information. The fear of collaboration is mostly driven by competitive fears, data privacy concerns, and proprietary orientations that limit opportunities for cross-organizational learning and innovation. While it is clear that the transition to an inter- and trans-firewall paradigm is not easy, we feel it will continue to grow and at some point it will become a key weapon, available for decisions scientists to drive disruptive value and efficiencies.

R&D Approach Helps Adopt New Technology

In almost every corporate annual report you will find that executives make innovation one of their top priorities for their respective firm. Business analytics can certainly help a company embrace innovation and steer direction by leveraging critical data and acting on the results. For example, a market research executive analyzing customer and market data to anticipate new product features that will attract new customers.

There is another angle on innovation for business analytics that pertains to how companies keep on top of the new analytic technology that can make an impact on their business. For many legitimate reasons, organizations find it hard to make changes after spending years implementing a data management, BI, and analytic stack. We've also seen a lot of wars being fought when someone prefers their own flavor of technology because they see the technology brand as a vital part of their skill set. So the question is, how can you stay on top of this and at the same time minimize risk and ensure that personal preference doesn't get in the way?

We sat down with the CIO of R&DVP Technology Strategy & Innovation at Visa Inc., Joe Cunningham, to discuss this topic. Visa's R&D organization forms part of Joe's function with Visa's Global Technology division. Cunningham made it a point to start off by saying that his R&D organization has a "small r and big D." He means that his team's goals are less about the research and more about the application of technology. His technology portfolio covers a wide range of technologies, such as authentication and fraud systems. Big Data analytics are certainly a key part of his portfolio and one that his team applies a lot of rigor to, to ensure that they stay on top of analytic innovation.

When people think about R&D, they often stereotype them as people that build cool stuff—but sometimes it has nothing to do with that. For example, a key role that Joe's team plays for his organization relates to education and corporate communications.

In this case, Cunningham's team will be asked to look both internally and externally to ensure that the organization is applying as much rigor to the question as possible. The team will then present the results internally in order to brief his colleagues. Additionally, this research will be sent to corporate communications in order for them to convey the firm's stance on the issue.

There are two core programs within Joe Cunningham's team:

Program	Goal	Core Elements
Innovation management	Tap into the latent creativity of all Visa employees, providing them with a platform to demonstrate mastery and engage collaboratively with their colleagues.	Employee personal growth Employee acquisition and retention
Research and open innovation	Look outside of the company and scan the environment for trends, new technology, and approaches	Innovation Competitive advantage

Adding Big Data Technology into the Mix

Cunningham's team at Visa took different approaches to bring Apache Hadoop into Visa that were dependent upon the business area. We asked Cunningham to outline their process as many enterprises are struggling with where to get started with Big Data technology.

1. **Practical approach.** Start with problem and then find a solution.
2. **Opportunistic approach.** Start with technology and then find a home for it.

   For both approaches, the team conducted the following activities:

   a. **Play.** R&D team members may request to install the technology in their lab to get more familiar with the technology.

   b. **Initial business review.** Talk with business owner to validate the applicability and rank the priorities to ensure that it is worth pursuing any further. *Note:* The business owner may in fact be IT too!

   c. **Architecture review.** Assess the validity of the underling architecture and ensure that it maps to IT's standards.

   d. **Pilot use cases.** Find a use case to test the technology out.

   e. **Transfer from R&D to PRODUCTION.** Negotiate internally regarding what it would take to move it from research to production using the following table:

Who needs to be involved in this process?

Operations	Nonfunctional integration	How does this integrate with our existing programs? (Monitoring, security, intrusion, etc.)
Engineering	Readiness	What do we need to do to prepare from a skill and infrastructure perspective to take on this project? Liaise with application development to determine if they leverage an existing program, buy, or build.
Application development	Functional requirements	How does this new technology map to the business functional requirements?
Business users	Derived value	How can new technology solve business problems I have or anticipate? How can I find new business opportunities?

Joe Cunningham explains that innovation comes from outside the corporate wall of one institution:

> We have a lot of smart people, but there are other smart people out there too. We want to be exposed to the value they are creating. You can be opportunistic to find things, but you can also be systematic. We have a systematic program here that formalizes relationships with a powerful ecosystem [shown in the table following].

Innovation ecosystem: Leveraging brain power from outside of your organization

Source	Example
Academic community	Tap into a major university who did a major study on social network analytics.
Vendors research arms	Leverage research a vendor completed in their labs demonstrating success leveraging unstructured data.
Research houses	Use research content to support a given hypothesis for a new endeavor.
Government agencies	Discuss fraud strategies with the intelligence community.
Venture capital orgs	Have a venture capital firm review some new trends they are tracking and investing in.
Start-ups	Invite BI and analytic technology start-ups in instead of just sticking with the usual suspects.

Big Data Technology Terms

Big Data as an industry is very nascent and new technologies and terms pop up on a weekly basis. This fast-paced environment is fueled by the open-source community, emerging technology companies, and industry Goliaths such as IBM, Oracle, SAP, SAS, and Teradata. Needless to say, it's hard to create a definitive list of terms that will have any longevity. Given that caveat, here is a mini Big Data glossary:

Term	Definition
Algorithm	Math that is used to analyze data. In general, a procedure for calculations; a list of instructions to calculate a function. In software, the actual implementation of such a procedure in a programming language.
Analytics	Using math to derive meaning from data.
Analytics Platform	A set of analytic tools and computational power used to query and process data.
Appliance	Optimized hardware and software purpose built for a specific set of activities.
Avro	Apache Avro is a data serialization system that allows for encoding the schema of Hadoop files. It is proficient at parsing data. Part of the Apache Hadoop project.
Batch	A job or process that runs in the background without human interaction.
Big Data	The de facto standard definition of big data is data that goes beyond the traditional limits of data along three dimensions: volume, variety, velocity. The combination of these three dimensions makes the data more complex to ingest, process, and visualize.
Big Insights	IBM's commercial distribution of Hadoop with enterprise class value added components.
Cassandra	An open-source columnar database managed by the Apache Software Foundation.
Clojure	Pronounced "closure." A dynamic programming language based on LISP (which was the de facto artificial programming language from late 1950s). Typically used for parallel data processing.
Cloud	General term used to refer to any computing resources—software, hardware or service—that is delivered as a service over a network.
Cloudera	The first commercial distributor of Hadoop. Cloudera provides enterprise-class value-added components with the Hadoop distribution.
Columnar Database	The storing and optimizing of data by columns. Particularly useful for some analytics processing that uses data based on a column.

(Continued)

Term	Definition
Complex Event Processing (CEP)	A process that analyzes and acts upon the events as they occur in real-time.
Data Mining	The process of discovering patterns, trends, and relationships from data using machine learning.
Distributed Processing	The execution of a program across multiple CPUs.
Dremel	Dremel is a scalable, interactive ad-hoc query system for analysis and is capable of running aggregation queries over trillion-row tables in seconds.
Flume	Flume is a framework for populating Hadoop data from Web servers, application servers, mobile devices, etc.
Grid	Loosely coupled servers networked together to process workloads in parallel.
Hadapt	A commercial provider that offers a relational add-on for Hadoop where data is moved between HDFS and relational tables via a high speed connector.
Hadoop	An open-source project framework that can store large unstructured data (HDFS) and processes the unstructured data (MapReduce) in a cluster of computers (grid).
HANA	An in-memory processing computing platform from SAP that is designed for high-volume transaction and real-time analytics.
Hbase	A distributed, columnar NoSQL database.
HDFS	The Hadoop File System, which is the storage mechanism for Hadoop.
Hive	A SQL-like query language for Hadoop.
Horton Works	A commercial distribution of Hadoop with enterprise-class value-added components.
HPC	High-performance computing. Used colloquially to refer to devices designed for high-speed floating point processing, in-memory with some disk parallelization.
HStreaming	A commercial add-on for Hadoop that provides real-time CEP processing.
Machine learning	An algorithmic technique for learning from empirical data and then using those lessons to predict future outcomes of new data.
Mahout	An Apache project to create a library of scalable, machine-learning algorithms for Hadoop mostly implemented in MapReduce.
MapR	A commercial distribution of Hadoop with enterprise-class value-added components.

Term	Definition
MapReduce	A parallel computational batch processing frame for Hadoop where jobs are mostly written in Java. The job breaks up a larger problem into smaller pieces of work and distributes the workload across the grid so that jobs can be worked on simultaneously (mapper). A master job (reducer) collects all the interim results and combines them.
Massively Parallel Processing (MPP)	A system (operating system, processors, and memory) that coordinates simultaneous program execution.
MPP Appliance	An integrated platform with processors, memory, disk, and software to process workloads in parallel.
MPP Database	A database that has been optimized for an MPP environment.
MongoDB	A scalable, high-performance, open source NoSQL database written in C++.
NoSQL Database	A term for any type of database that does not use SQL for the primary retrieval of data from the database. NoSQL databases have limited traditional functionality and are designed for scalability and high-performance retrieve and append. Typically, NoSQL databases store data as key-value pairs, which works well for data that is unrelated in nature.
Oozie	Oozie is a workflow processing system that lets users define a series of jobs written in languages—such as Map Reduce, Pig, and Hive.
Pig	A distributed processing framework that uses a query language (Pig Latin) to perform data transformations. Pig Latin programs are currently translated into MapReduce jobs for execution on Hadoop.
R	R is an open-source language and environment for statistical computing and graphics.
Real-Time	Today it is colloquially defined as immediate processing. Real-time processing originated in 1950s when multi-tasking machines provided the capability to "interrupt" a task for a higher priority task to be executed. These types of machines powered the space program, military applications, and many commercial control systems.
Relational Database	The storing and optimizing of data by rows and columns.
Scoring	Using a predictive model to predict future outcomes of new data.
Semi-structured Data	Unstructured data that can be put into a structure by available format descriptions.
Spark	A high-performance processing framework for in-memory analytic computational processing that is often used for real-time querying.
SQL (structured Query Language)	The language for storing, accessing, and manipulating data in a relational database.

(Continued)

Term	Definition
Sqoop	SQL-to-Hadoop is a command-line tool for capabilities such as importing individual tables or entire databases to files in Hadoop.
Storm	Open-source framework for distributed, fault-tolerant, real-time analytic processing.
Structured Data	Data that has a pre-set format.
Unstructured Data	Data that has no preset structure.
Whirr	Apache Whirr is a set of libraries for running cloud services.
YARN	YARN is the next generation computing framework in Apache Hadoop with support for programming paradigms besides MapReduce.

Data Size 101

Data is measured by basic units of measure that work up from a bit. A bit is represented by either a 1 (electricity flowing) or a 0 (no electricity flowing). This is called *binary code*. The code converts images, text, and sounds into numbers in order to send information from one digital device such as a computer to another.

Computers use binary numbers because they are easier to handle. In binary, the digits (read and write) are worth 1, 2, 4, 8, and so on—not units, tens, and hundreds. A byte is a unit of measure and it is 8 bits put together. In ordinary numbers, "1,001" is one unit. But in binary, "1001" is one 1, no 2, no 4, and one 8, which equals 9.

Sample ASCII Code: character to binary code

0 = 0011 0000	A = 0100 0001
1 = 0011 0001	B = 0100 0001
2 = 0011 0010	C = 0100 0001
3 = 0011 0011	D = 0100 0001
4 = 0011 0100	E = 0100 0001
5 = 0011 0101	F = 0100 0001
6 = 0011 0110	G = 0100 0001
7 = 0011 0111	H = 0100 0001
8 = 0011 1000	I = 0100 0001
9 = 0011 1001	J = 0100 0001

Table 3.1 shows the units of measure and some typical data represented by that unit of measure.

Table 3.1 How Data Is Measured

Unit of Measure	Approximate Size	Mathematical Representation	Examples
KB = kilobyte	1,000 (10^3 or one thousand) bytes	2^{10} or 1024 bytes	A typical joke = 1KB
MB = megabyte	1,000,000 (10^6 or one million) bytes	2^{20} or 1,048,576 bytes	Complete work of Shakespeare = 5MB
GB = gigabyte	1,000,000,000 (10^9 or one billion) bytes	2^{30} or 1,073,741,824 bytes	Ten yards of books on a shelf = 1GB
TB = terabyte	1,000,000,000,000 (or 10^{12})	2^{40} or 1,099,511,627,776 bytes	All the X-rays for a large hospital = 1TB Tweets; created daily = 12+TB; U.S. Library of Congress = 235TB
PB = petabyte	1,000,000,000,000,000 (or 10^{15})	2^{50} or 1,125,899,906,842,624 bytes	All U.S. academic research libraries = 2PB Data processed in a day by Google = 24PB
EB = exabyte	1,000,000,000,000,000,000 (or 10^{18})	2^{60} or 1,152,921,504,606,846,976 bytes	Total data created in 2006 = 161EB
ZB = zettabyte	1,000,000,000,000,000,000,000 (or 10^{21})	2^{70} or 1,180,591,620,717,411,303,424 bytes	Total amount of global data expected to be 2.7 ZB by end of 2012
YB = yottabyte	1,000,000,000,000,000,000,000,000 (or 10^{24})	2^{80} or 1,208,925,819,614,629,174,706,176	Today, to save all those bytes you need a data center as big as the state of Delaware

Source: "Total Amount of Global Data 2.7 Zettabytes," idc.com, December 1, 2010.

Notes

1. Chris Stolte, Dan Jewett, and Pat Hanrahan, "A New Approach: Rapid Fire Business Intelligence," Tableau Software, January 2011, www.tableausoftware.com/whitepapers/rapid-fire-business-intelligence.
2. Tasso Argyros, "We Did It Again! Another First—Business Analyst Direct Access to Hadoop Data," *Teradata Aster Data Blog*, June 2012, www.asterdata.com/blog/2012/06/12/we-did-it-again-another-first-business-analyst-direct-access-to-hadoop-data-3/.
3. W. Chan Kim and Renée Mauborgne, *Blue Ocean Strategy* (Cambridge, MA: Harvard Business School Press, 2005).
4. Margaret Rouse, "Software as a Service BI (SaaS BI)," SearchBusinessAnalytics, June 2012, http://searchbusinessanalytics.techtarget.com/definition/Software-as-a-Service-BI-SaaS-BI.
5. Ibid.

CHAPTER 4

Information Management

nformation management is a combination of the foundation and the plumbing in a house. Who wants to think about information management? Not many. But just like a house, if the foundation isn't solid, you'll have all sorts of structural problems that can cause it to come crashing down. Or, at least, you'll experience annoying problems that limit your abilities to live comfortably. Just like when you contract to have a house built, you want to invest in experienced builders who know how to build the foundation to meet today's needs and anticipate future needs so you'll have the ability to easily expand.

The Big Data Foundation

Just like the house analogy, the Big Data foundation is composed of two major systems. The first stores the data and the second processes it.

Big Data storage is often synonymously interchanged with the Hadoop File System (HDFS), but traditional data warehouses can also house Big Data. HDFS is distributed data storage that has become the de facto standard because you can store any type of data without limitations on the type or amount of data. One of the reasons HDFS has become so popular is that you don't have to do any "set up" to store the data. In traditional databases, you need to do quite a bit of "set up" in order to store data. You have to understand the data that will be housed in the database and set up the database by creating a schema. The schema is the blueprint for how you'll place data into tables with columns. The schema also contains rules about the data being stored—for example, which column(s) will be used to find or index the data in a particular table. With HDFS, you don't set up a blueprint; you simply dump the data into a file. Think about it as cutting and pasting all your data into a huge Microsoft Word file. This approach makes sense for massive quantities of data when the *value* of that data is *unknown*. After all, why would you pay an architect to put together a blueprint if you don't know that you're building a house?

Another reason HDFS is used to complement traditional data warehouses are due to limitations on the type of data the database supports and the size of data that the database can store. Often, traditional databases "support" the data type but make it impractical to manipulate the data once it is stored thereby rendering it fairly useless.

Big Data processing involves the manipulation and calculations that occur on the Big Data. Traditional databases have differing abilities to process Big Data sets effectively and efficiently. Additionally, there is a wide degree of variance in how database software exploits the underlying hardware architecture. Database software that is hardware agnostic doesn't take full advantage of the underlying hardware architecture. But some database software is tightly coupled with the hardware architecture so as to exploit the unique hardware processing capabilities to get throughput processing. Data warehouse appliances fall into this category and have varying degrees of performance advantages due to this tight coupling.

Today, the de facto processing software for HDFS is MapReduce, which was discussed in the previous chapter. MapReduce is a fault-tolerant parallel programming framework that was designed to harness distributed processing capabilities. MapReduce automatically divides the processing workload into smaller workloads that are distributed. When working with HDFS, data manipulation and calculations are programmed using the MapReduce framework in the language of choice (typically Java programming language).

A "parallel computing framework" is meaningless to most of us, so let's draw an analogy to something we can relate to. For example, a factory with 10 assembly lines receives an order to create 500 toy trucks. One assembly line could create all 500 toy trucks or, alternatively, there could be a division of labor among the assembly lines where each assembly line produces 50 toy trucks. If each assembly line started at the same time and everything went flawlessly each assembly line would complete their production of 50 trucks simultaneously. This efficient division of labor was fairly straightforward because each toy truck could be produced *independently*. However, if three of the assembly lines could only produce the engine and the remaining seven assembly lines could only produce the balance of the toy truck the division of labor becomes more complicated. In this scenario, planning has to take into account that there is a *dependency* between the engine production and rest of the toy truck production.

Just like in the toy truck production, some data manipulation and calculations can be performed independently. To maximize the processing throughput, MapReduce assumes that the workloads being distributed are independent tasks and the workload is equally divided just like the division of labor to the 10 assembly lines to produce 50 trucks each. However, if there are dependencies in the processing workload, the MapReduce framework is unaware of those dependencies. The programmer has to be aware of those dependencies and has to specifically divide the workload up in the program understanding that MapReduce will automatically distribute tasks. This type of programming is called *parallel programming*. Just like the production planning that has to occur in dividing the workload between assembly lines that only produce engines and all the other assembly lines was more complicated, parallel programming is more complicated. One of the benefits of MapReduce and some data warehouse appliances is that the easier independent processing is automatically handled by the framework or date warehouse appliance.

MapReduce was designed to be fault tolerant because, when using unknown hardware whose reliability is unknown, there needs to be a way to gracefully handle processing failure. Fault tolerant software is designed to automatically recover and handle processing failures, which makes it highly reliable. MapReduce along with many data warehouse appliances are fault tolerant.

There are a few different typical workflows that become processing bottlenecks as data gets increasingly larger. The first one is the speed of ingesting or loading the data. The second one is the speed of analytics computational processing (or "number crunching" as it's often referred to). The third is the speed at which you can perform your analytics on-demand and respond to the business.

For example, the data may be machine-generated, creating relentless volumes of data and the speed at which the data is being created may make it difficult to consume. If you're trying to act on the data or analyze the data as it's being generated that may be difficult. Let's take a real-world example, algorithmic trading, to illustrate the bottlenecks. For algorithmic trading, real-time analytics analyze and act upon the data as it is generated and streaming by on the wire.

Let's say you were looking at tick trading data and you're making new trades based on the tick trading data. As the data is flying by, there could be real-time analytics that are processing on each individual transaction as it is occurring in real-time. Those actions are making decisions and triggering events such as buys, sells, or shorts. In the past, much of that real-time transactional data was either not captured or captured substantially afterward for analysis long after the real-time event unfolded. Now, the real-time streaming data is acted upon in real-time and then pushed into some type of Big Data storage—a data warehouse appliance or HDFS. There, the transactional data is stored in its native, raw format and is analyzed overtime to help improve the analytics and actions that unfold in real-time. The faster and more often you can perform this cycle on the transactional data the faster your organization learns and improves.

Big Data Computing Platforms (or Computing Platforms That Handle the Big Data Analytics Tsunami)

While there are many different computing techniques available today, parallel computing platforms are the only platforms suited to handle the speed and volume of data being produced today.

There are three prominent parallel computing options available today:

1. Clusters or grids
2. Massively parallel processing (MPP)
3. High performance computing (HPC)

Clusters and grids are types of computing where servers are loosely coupled and networked together for distributing workloads. Clusters or grid environments can be either homogeneous or heterogeneous commodity hardware environments. People tend to use cluster or grid approaches because the perceived total cost of ownership is negligible, since they can buy commodity hardware and pull it together. Grid environments do provide lower-cost storage but the price differential between a grid and other parallel alternatives is not as significant when you take a total cost of ownership perspective, as there are human costs to factor into setting up and maintaining the grid.

A variation on the cluster or grid is a public cloud environment, where a vendor such as Amazon or EC2 has set up a cluster or grid and sells space and computing power to customers via the Internet. Cloud environments have become popular for a few reasons. One is that they are "elastic," which means that I pay as I grow/shrink or only pay for the space/processing that I need today and, as my data/processing needs increase/decrease, I buy more or less from the vendor. The downside to cloud environments for Big Data is that at some point, the time it takes to get data to the cloud becomes longer and that may not be acceptable for the particular business requirement. Private clouds are a grid internal to an organization. Typically, private clouds are a "shared" environment where several business units share the cost of the Big Data infrastructure and support.

Massively parallel processing platforms are essentially a grid inside of a box. MPP platforms combine storage, memory, and compute to create a platform. Typically, MPP platforms are used for *known* high-value use cases. EMC Greenplum and ParAccel are examples of MPP platforms.

MPP appliances place the storage, memory, and compute into a single machine that is optimized for performance and scalability. In an appliance, the network that connects the storage and compute is designed for optimal throughput. MPP appliances go one step further to design the software for the specific MPP platform, which allows the software to maximize the storage and computational capabilities of the MPP device. MPP appliances have been used in enterprises for 10+ years and with that maturity the software is designed to be easier to use for analytics. While you can typically write your own parallel programs to embed analytics into the platform (the equivalent of writing Mappers and Reducers) you don't have to because there are a variety of easier to use tools available on MPP appliances. Typically, these tools automatically perform the parallel processing under the covers. This makes it easier to use and delivers on performance and scalability. MPP appliances are designed for price performance. Examples of MPP appliances are IBM Netezza (just recently renamed IBM PureData System for Analytics) and Teradata.

The next option is a high-performance computing option, or HPC environment. HPC environments are designed for high-speed floating point processing and much of the calculations are done in memory, which renders the highest computational performance possible. Cray Computers and IBM Blue Gene are examples of HPC environments. HPC environments are predominantly used by research organizations and by business units that demand very high scalability and computational performance, where the value being created is so huge and strategic that cost is not the most important consideration. While HPC environments have been around for quite some time, they are used for specialty applications and primarily provide a programming environment for custom application development.

Big Data Computation

Big Data computing platforms are all parallel computing environments that require some type of parallel programming. Parallel programming is another order of magnitude more difficult than standard programming. In a parallel computing environment, you have to think about how to you structure your code in a way that when the workload is distributed to the parallel computing processors, the results are combined to produce the correct result. The various Big Data computing platform vendors have varied approaches to the level of effort involved in parallel programming. Some environments provide software layers or tools to make it easier while others simply provide standard programming tools, and the hard work to do the parallel programming is left to the skill and experience of the programmer. The typical parallel computing environments include:

- MapReduce
- In-database analytics
- Message passing interface (MPI)

Before we investigate these techniques, let's understand the difficulty with programming in a parallel compute environment.

To illustrate the work involved with parallel programming, let's use two simple calculations as examples: average and median. The math in both of these calculations is straightforward but parallelizing the activities to compute the math gets complicated in one of these calculations.

Average, as you know, is just taking all the numbers that you have in a list and then adding them up and dividing by the total number of numbers that were in that list to find out what the average is among those numbers. Median is taking a list of numbers and finding the middle number in that list. Average is simple to compute in a parallel environment and median is not.

In a parallel compute environment, each processor has memory to use in computations of data that the processor is associated with. To help in understanding, let's say that the parallel compute environment has 100 processors. The average calculation gets passed to each of the 100 processors. Each processor calculates the average of the data that processor is associated with, which results in 100 interim subtotals. Each of the subtotals is passed to a master or controller to perform the final average calculation by averaging all the 100 interim subtotals. The workload could be evenly divided by all the available processors because each of the subtotals was independent of each other.

However, median is not a calculation that easily lends itself well to a parallel compute environment. Again, each of the 100 processors sees part of the list. All 100 processors can find the middle number of the numbers it has visibility to and can return that middle number back to the master controller. Those interim middle numbers can be used by the master controller to determine the middle number. However, that final middle number will not be the middle number of the entire list! In order to determine the median, the list of numbers needs to be sorted and then redistributed across the processors or each of the processors needs to be able to communicate with the other processors to correctly locate the middle number of the entire list.

Let's take a look at how MapReduce, a common parallelization technique used with Big Data, works. MapReduce is typically used in conjunction with HDFS but there are also implementations of MapReduce for data warehouses. In the MapReduce framework, a master controller distributes work via a Mapper function to all of the available processors. Each of the processors independently performs the Mapper task and the results are fed into a Reducer task, which summarizes the work from Mappers. Today, the Mappers and Reducers are custom code written in Java. However, there are higher-level tools and analytics available that use MapReduce under the covers. For example, Pig and Hive are two open-source tools that provide a SQL-like interface to HDFS because sometimes it's easier to use SQL than to custom code the same capability that is inherent in SQL. There are other open-source projects such as Mahout and Lucene, which are evolving libraries of analytic functions that are typically written in MapReduce.

The second software parallelization technique is an overloaded term called in-database analytics. There are two ways the term is used. The first is to refer to the collection of SQL language extension capabilities called *user-defined extensions* that take custom code and execute the code in database. The second are prebuilt, parallelized analytics that execute in the database. Both of these methods move the computational processing next to the data where the data resides so that you avoid all of the latency and performance bottlenecks associated with moving Big Data.

There are three types of user-defined extensions defined by the SQL language:

1. *User-defined function* (UDF), which performs a task and returns one value
2. *User-defined aggregate* (UDA), which summarizes a group of data and returns one value
3. *User-defined table function* (UDTF), which takes data of one shape (i.e., 10 columns and 100 rows) and reshapes the output (i.e., 2 columns and 552 rows)

In a parallel data warehouse, SQL along with user-defined extensions are executed in parallel automatically without having to explicitly perform the parallel programming. However, just like in MapReduce, a programmer who is writing a user-defined extension needs to understand how to program calculations such as median even though SQL automatically distributes the workload. Mappers are equivalent to UDTFs and Reducers are equivalent to UDAs.

Prebuilt in-database analytics leverage user-defined extensions to encapsulate analytic functions such as linear regression, decision trees, and many other analytic functions. In this method, the parallel programming has already been performed and the analytic function can simply be invoked to perform the specified task. Examples of out-of-box, prebuilt, in-database analytics are included in IBM Netezza, DB Lytix by Fuzzy Logix, and Alpine Data Miner.

Parallel-compute environments are shared nothing environments whereby design, each processor, and its associated memory are unaware of the other processors. The third software parallelization technique is message passing interface, which is interprocess communication software to facilitate sharing of information between processors in a shared nothing compute environment. This is a collection of software processes that allow a distributed environment to share information between the processors. For the median calculation, MPI is used to share interim processing results between the processors while attempting to find the middle number.

Each parallel-compute platform uses one or more of these software parallelization techniques. It's very typical for HPC environments to use MPI, it's very typical for MPP environments to use in-database analytics, and it's very typical for grids to use MapReduce. But there are hybrid approaches as well. For example, IBM Netezza has an in-database MapReduce capability, MPI capability, and both in-database analytic capabilities while Teradata Aster has a SQLMR capability.

More on Big Data Storage

As mentioned earlier, Big Data storage is often used interchangeably with HDFS. However, data warehouse have been used for Big Data storage of known value for quite some time and have evolved to several storage techniques. By far the most common and popular is the relational database that stores information in rows and columns. In relational databases the primary access is via the row. Another storage technique is a columnar storage scheme. While a columnar database has rows and columns, information is predominantly accessed via the columns. There are also hybrid approaches that allow for some information to be easily accessed via row and other data to be easily accessed via columns. Examples of relational data warehouses include IBM Netezza, Teradata, and Oracle Exadata. Vertica [an HP company] is the most prevalent columnar storage data warehouse.

Big Data Computational Limitations

With all the Big Data buzz and gee whiz bang technology available today, you might conclude that there are no limitations to processing Big Data but laws of physics still apply. The typical Big Data computing platform limitations encountered are:

- Disk bound
- I/O bound
- Memory bound
- CPU bound

Disk bound means you simply don't have enough storage capacity (e.g., have 2 PB of data and there is only 500 TB of storage capacity).

I/O bound is when there isn't enough bandwidth to move around the data to meet the needs of the business. Think about this as having a pipe with a 10-inch diameter and trying to squeeze 50 TB of Big Data through the pipe in five minutes in order to provide the service level agreements (SLAs) that your business requires when it would take a 100-inch pipe to meet the SLAs.

Computational platforms use a combination of memory and CPUs to process Big Data analytics. Memory is like the scrap of paper we use when doing a more complicated math problem. Most analytic software today attempts to load all the data needed for a calculation into memory and then uses the CPU to perform the calculation. This technique is very fast but is bounded by the available memory. Memory is limited on various computing platforms because memory is still fairly expensive. There are heavy in-memory systems, such as SAP Hana, which are quickly becoming cost effective solutions. Here is the typical scenario when an analytic process become memory bound:

Let's say you had 500 TBs of data and you're running an analytic across 100 TBs. As the analytic computation performs, it's trying to shove 100 TBs into memory do to the necessary crunching. The analytic process may get to 90 TBs and then become bounded by the available memory on the computing platform, which means the analytic process can't perform its task.

Your Big Data analytic hit the proverbial wall. When that happens, data scientists and programmers perform unnatural acts to process the data. Often, they will spend a lot of time trying to figure out how to break apart their problem to process smaller amounts of the data and then use that in combination to get to the end result. Or they might use a sample of the data and perhaps extrapolate or estimate the end results. These activities can become very arduous and time consuming and result in a limited analysis instead of the intended analysis. For example, a forecast may be limited to using only 12 months of data to create a forecast. This may seem inconsequential but if there is a three-year cycle that occurs, the forecast won't realize that pattern exists and will produce an inaccurate forecast.

Similarly, some analytics are more computationally intensive, which means that they use more of the capacity of the CPU. An example of a mathematically intensive analytic is Monte Carlo simulation. When executing a Monte Carlo simulation, a calculation or set of calculations are being performed with different starting conditions or parameters. In this huge "what-if" process, there are many computational intensive calculations being performed concurrently that can simply overwhelm and exhaust the CPU capacity.

Big Data Emerging Technologies

For computing platforms, some of the interesting and unique emerging technologies are the potential use for solid-state drives, or SSD drives, in place of hard drives that are common today. Solid-state drives are memory devices that will allow you to *persist* data. SSD is sometimes called flash-memory, which refers to the underlying chips used in this technology. SSD drives are the equivalent of thumb drives. These drives have many performance advantages. For a solid-state drive, the start-up or spin-up time is almost instantaneous.

The random access time to get to any information on a SSD is typically 5 to 10 times faster than it would be on a hard drive. The latency in which data is actually read is greatly reduced because a hard drive is a mechanical device and a SSD is not. SSD is still emerging because the price ($/TB) today is still costly. Another issue with SSD is the write longevity. On a traditional hard drive, data can be written to the disk almost in perpetuity. With solid state drives, there is typically a limit in terms of the number of overwrites that can be performed.

As SSD becomes more affordable and the write longevity is addressed, this will become the prevalent storage for performance, low-latency-oriented Big Data analytics processing.

The other really promising technology analytics computation is *graphical processing units* (GPUs). GPGPU, which is a general-purpose GPU, is the emerging technology being explored for Big Data computing platforms, while GPUs are used in PCs for video processing. The GPGPU is an adapted form that can be used for general purpose types of applications. GPGPUs are mostly used for vector processing, which is commonly used when performing Big Data analytics. This is very interesting commodity-based technology, whose hardware is manufactured by NVIDIA and ATI, that provides similar computational capabilities to the floating point processing typically only available in HPC environments. Adoption of GPUs has been slow because it requires fairly low level programming in either C or *compute unified device architecture* (CUDA). CUDA, developed by NVDIA, is an extension to the C programming language (C API) that facilitates the execution of C programs on CUDA compliant GPUs.

Today, banks are experimenting with GPU grids for large-scale computationally intensive workloads. For example, banks are using GPU grids to perform large-scale Monte Carlo simulations across 10 million portfolios with hundreds of thousands of simulations. That kind of computation is either impossible or simply takes too long in a traditional environment. So, while the ticket to entry for Big Data is no data movement, in computationally intensive Big Data problems such as this, the overhead associated with moving the data is dwarfed by the computational speed up that is gained by moving the data to this very high speed computation. After the calculations are performed, the results are typically shipped back to the traditional environment for persistent storage. Fuzzy Logix offers a GPU appliance that does not include Big Data persistent but augments Big Data storage.

CHAPTER 5

Business Analytics

The future is here, and now, at your disposal to capitalize on. Today, we are at an inflection point at which we have the intellectual and computational power to fully capitalize on and ride a wave to *cost effective* top-line revenue growth powered by Big Data analytics. Will you take some plunges and wipe out along the way? Absolutely! But the sooner you start learning, the sooner you'll get to ride that perfect wave, which will create a friction-free environment for your business to reap the huge financial rewards awaiting those who master the perfect wave.

Predictive analytics in the past has been largely constrained so much so that many of the constraints became well-entrenched assumptions that were the shackles that constrained the potential results. Even so, those who have used predictive analytics have realized significant, quantifiable business value. In this new age of Big Data analytics, the assumptions have been cast aside as Big Data is disrupting the well-known but not fully realized discipline of predictive analytics.

The term *predictive analytics* was coined to distinguish statistics from more advanced type of calculations that are used to predict likelihoods of future outcomes. Certain industries, such as banks, insurance companies, and digital advertising, have fully embraced predictive analytics but most other businesses are still at very early stages of adoption. While there is a full spectrum of analytics for Big Data analytics the emphasis will be to use the descriptive statistics in the Big Data exploratory stage when the value of the data isn't yet known and move toward the predictive and prescriptive analytics stages as value becomes known or discovered (see Figure 5.1).

Big Data analytics uses predictive and prescriptive analytics and is changing the analytics landscape. While descriptive statistics, initially made popular by SAS and SPSS, describe what has happened in the past, predictive analytics uses the past information to predict future outcomes with some degree of likelihood. Prescriptive analytics takes that past information and uses it to direct future activities to achieve optimal or near optimal results. While each of these types of techniques has been used for decades there are major shifts

Descriptive Analytics (Business Intelligence)	Predictive Analytics	Prescriptive Analytics
o What and when did it happen? o How much is impacted and how often does it happen? o What is the problem?	o What is likely to happen next? o What if these trends continue? o What if?	o What is the best answer? o What is the best outcome given uncertainty? o What are significantly differing and better choices?
Statistics	Data Mining Predictive Modeling Machine Learning Forecasting Simulation	Constraint-based optimization Multiobjective optimization Global optimization
Information Management		

Figure 5.1 Big Data Analytics

underway when these techniques are combined with Big Data. The major shifts are:

- Using all or more of the data to create a predictive model
- Combining multiple analytic models and techniques to improve the results
- Creating a closed loop where new learnings are used to adapt the production models
- Using the predictive models in as close to real time as possible
- Focusing on applying predictive model techniques (a.k.a. algorithms) rather than inventing new techniques

For those organizations that develop Big Data analytic solutions there is the potential to realize unprecedented business value but you need new skills to be able to capitalize on the shifts. You'll need data scientists who are adept at visualizing large data and discerning between signal and noise. These data scientists will need to have deep math and computer science skills. They'll also have to be open minded and willing to try new things and fail quickly. They'll need the ability to quickly incorporate learnings from previous failures to try new models and techniques. And most important, they'll need to understand your business or have the listening skills to be able to learn from those in your business that knows your business and industry well.

Let's take a look at some of those critical skills and how that relates to successfully and effectively deploying Big Data analytics.

The Last Mile in Data Analysis

You cannot chat with Dr. Usama Fayyad for very long without the term "last mile" coming up in the conversation. Here's what he means, in his own words:

> Let's say you process the data, you run the best algorithms on it using the best infrastructure and you do all sorts of acrobatics. Now you face the most difficult question: How do you use the results of your efforts to deliver value to the business unit?
>
> The "last mile" is a group of people who are basically there to deliver the results of the analysis and put them in terms that the business can understand. This "last mile" group is made up of data analysts who know enough about the business to present to the CMO or the CEO. You need experienced data analysts who aren't afraid to get their hands dirty.
>
> It's not easy to find and hire those people. And in many companies, they are quickly turned into tactical resources. That's a mistake, because these are people who can help develop and guide strategy, move the needle, and grapple with big issues.
>
> At Yahoo!, we created a lot of controversy. People accused us of being wasteful. They said, "How can you just sit there and just think strategy?" But we created some of the biggest value drivers for the company by addressing these big needles that never get addressed if you go about them tactically.
>
> A very quick example that I can talk about publicly is Yahoo! Mail, which is used by 250+ million people or more, worldwide. One of the things you will see when you log in is a news preview module. The news preview module became important because it helped us retain active users. People would sign up for a Yahoo! Mail account, but then they wouldn't use it.
>
> When we analyzed the data, we noticed something that I couldn't explain. The data was saying that new users like to read news when they read email. Don't ask me why. I can't explain it. By adding a news preview window to the new users of Yahoo! Mail, we were able to increase the return rate by 40%. And it turned out that in addition to new users, the entire population of users liked reading news while looking at their email. As a result, the news preview became one of the main features of Yahoo! Mail. To this day, I still can't explain why. But we know statistically it holds, and it made a huge difference to the business.
>
> Another story I'll share with you is how we built the behavioral targeting business at Yahoo! This business was designed for targeting

ads to users on what we believe are their interests as opposed to targeting ads the traditional way: based on the context of the pages the ads appear in. The power here is that pages where context is meaningful to ads is a small minority of page views (think about reading email or news). When I joined, it was a $20 million business. When I left, it was a half a billion dollar business, with essentially the same inventory and almost zero investment.

Here's what it was: We had something like 2,500 categories of interest per user. We were very proud of it. For any user, I can tell you 2,500 dimensions of what they're interested in. Nobody took the time to look at it very carefully, other than me. I asked, "Okay guys, where do these categories come from? How do they die away? How do they get managed? How confident are we that we're computing them correctly?"

One of the biggest controversial things I did was to reduce the categories from 2,500 to 300. People cried foul. They said, "How could you do this to us? You're the data guy!"

I basically said, "Guys, I can reduce the number of categories and guarantee the quality, make sure they're up to date, and make sure we're using the right algorithms. For example, after you buy a digital camera, you are no longer interested in seeing ads for digital cameras. You're done, you've already bought the camera, and you won't become interested again for another six months to a year.

But algorithms are going to continue targeting the hell out of you with digital cameras ads because you showed us signs that you were interested in digital cameras—even though the truth is that you won't be looking for cameras again for the next 6 to 12 months. If you buy a car, you probably won't be looking at cars for the next two years, so targeting you with car ads during that time will be counterproductive. Shoes are different. Some people will wait months before looking at shoes again, other people will continue shopping. The point is that your attributes aren't fixed, they change over time. Data analysts are the people who figure these things out. They help companies save money and make money.

In one sense, what he's saying echoes Georges Clemenceau's famous phrase "War is too important to be left to the generals." But what we really believe he's saying is that data should be perceived and treated as a critical asset, not as a cost of doing business. Data analytics—and in particular Big Data analytics—should be elevated to the senior management level and become the responsibility of C-level executives. When that happens, data analytics will have traveled the "last" and most important mile.

Now that we have a working definition for Big Data, let's define analytics a bit and then relate both back to our examples in marketing. Analytics is another broad term that is used to define an entire spectrum of computations—see Figure 5.1 for examples of analytics in various categories along the spectrum.

Many of these techniques started in statistics and were used in business intelligence dashboards and scorecards. BI helped us aggregate information about events that took place in the past. As valuable as BI is, it essentially provides us with a look in the rearview mirror. The colloquial definition of analytics is using past information to provide insights into the future, which essentially is like using the bright lights in the dark to look out ahead and anticipate what's coming down the road.

Now, if we combine massive amounts of data (a.k.a. Big Data) along with powerful analytics (a.k.a. advanced analytics) there is a greater deal of texture or context to predict future outcomes, which allows us to then take it to the next level of using those insights to automate actions or to provide a short list of actions that are likely to result in significantly improved outcomes.

Not only can the Big Data collected by the iPad or Kindle be used to create lift in marketing campaigns and used to drive promotional activities to drive higher customer lifetime value but it can also be used to innovate products that will meet latent demand. Can you imagine actually creating a product that you know will be successfully adopted in the market before you spend $1 on the research and development? Not only does that reduce your R&D costs but it also speeds your time to market.

Geospatial Intelligence Will Make Your Life Better

At this point, it's fair to say that we've assembled an all-star team of experts to share their thoughts on the most important and most relevant trends in Big Data analytics.

Even on an all-star team there are standout performers. Jeff Jonas certainly qualifies as a standout among all-stars, and we're gratified that he made the time to chat with us about a topic that's close to his heart. But first, here's some background about Jeff.

Jonas is an IBM Fellow and Chief Scientist of the IBM Entity Analytics Group. The IBM Entity Analytics Group was formed based on technologies developed by Systems Research & Development (SRD), founded by Jonas in 1984, and acquired by IBM in January, 2005.

Prior to the acquisition, Jonas lead SRD through the design and development of a number of unique systems including technology used by the Las Vegas gaming industry to make cheating more difficult. You've probably seen

Jonas' work featured in documentaries on the Discovery Channel and other networks.

Following an investment in 2001 by In-Q-Tel, the venture capital arm of the CIA, SRD began playing a role in America's national security and counterterrorism mission. One such contribution includes an analysis of the connections between the individual 9/11 terrorists. That analysis is now taught in universities and has been widely cited by think tanks and the media.

Jonas is a member of the Markle Foundation Task Force on National Security in the Information Age, a Board Member of the U.S. Geospatial Intelligence Foundation (USGIF), on the EPIC Advisory Board, on the Privacy International Advisory Board, a Senior Associate at the Center for Strategic and International Studies (CSIS), and a Distinguished Engineer of Information Systems (adjunct) at Singapore Management University. He periodically testifies on privacy and counterterrorism in such venues as the Department of Homeland Security's Data Privacy and Integrity Advisory Committee, and other federally convened commissions.

Jonas was briefly a quadriplegic in 1988 following a car accident. Today, he competes in Ironman triathlons around the world. As you can see, Jonas' legendary status extends beyond the world of business data. Here's a summary of what he shared with us in a recent conversation:

> More and more sensors are coming online generating higher and higher quality data about where things are when. As a result, there's a new form of analytics that is right now just beginning to mature. Those new analytics take advantage of data about where things are when (and how things move), and use that data for making extraordinarily high quality predictions.

The combined impact of those new analytics creates what Jeff describes as "geospatial intelligence." Simply put, geospatial intelligence is about using data about space and time to improve the quality of predictive analysis.

> You pull up your smartphone and you look at traffic and it shows you the streets highlighted in red and yellow. It's taking anonomized and aggregated motion data from people's phones and looking at their average speed of travel. Then it's helping you to avoid traffic, plain and simple. That's geospatial analytics today.

But this form of analytics is evolving very fast, says Jonas. Not too long from now, geospatial analytics will be considered a standard part of modern life:

Imagine searching for a drycleaner and getting a recommendation that isn't the closest drycleaner to your house, or even the closest to where you are right now, or the most popular drycleaner by user ratings. Imagine that instead of the typical search results, you get the name and address of a drycleaner that is on the precise route that you travel most frequently, and it's on the correct side of the road. And if there are two drycleaners nearby, it's going to tell you which one tends to be the least busy at the predicted time of your arrival. That's the promise of geospatial intelligence.

For advertisers, geospatial intelligence will mean the ads we see will feel less like spam and more like relevant information.

It's going to come from weaving together data that has traditionally not been woven together. It will combine stuff about you on Facebook with comments you've made recently on Twitter. When you weave all of that data together, the quality of the predictions get better and better. For example, Facebook knows I'm a triathlete. So I see an ad that says something like, "You're a triathlete. Do you want abs like this?" and it shows me a picture of some dude's perfect abs, and of course I want abs like that, so I might click on the ad.

But most likely, he will skip it. Now Jeff describes a scenario that's more likely to generate a positive outcome for the advertiser. Let's say that he's attending a business meeting in another part of the country, and he sees an ad for a triathlon coach near the hotel where he's staying. That ad is highly likely to grab his attention. What's the difference between the two ads? The ad for the triathlon coach is generated by a system that uses geospatial data and the ad for the great abs isn't.

From Jonas' perspective, geospatial data represents ultimate truth—it's based on what's really happening, where it's happening, and at the very moment that it's happening. Data doesn't get more real than that!

Here's a brief story that Jeff tells to illustrate the point:

Imagine two ladies sitting in front of you. They're identical twins. But they both say, "We're one person." Of course, you're sitting there with them and you see two separate individuals. But they are adamant about being one person. And the data—at least most of it—is on their side.

Their passports will show the same photo. Their fingerprints, their voiceprints, their irises, their DNA—all of the standard biometric tests—will support their version of the truth. Even their mother swears they are one person. But you're sitting there and you know they are lying, no matter what the data tells you.

By now, says Jonas, you're starting to feel a little confused. You might think, "Maybe they are one person, and I'm going crazy . . ." But then you remember there's a sure way to prove they are two people. Hand each of the twins a mobile phone with a GPS app. Each phone will show a slightly different location. Case closed. That's why proponents of geospatial intelligence call it the ultimate truth, the realest form of reality.

For competitive organizations, this isn't mere sophistry. This represents incredible value. Let's end this section of the book with Jeff's take on the future of predictive analytics:

> Real-time streaming analytics and geospatial intelligence will be essential for competitive businesses. When you make higher quality decisions faster and more consistently than your competitors, you win. You are more efficient, you deliver your products and services at lower cost, and your customers are happier.

Jeff is an inspiration on many levels, and we are honored to include his perspective in our book.

Listening: Is It Signal or Noise?

As data gets larger, it become increasingly difficult to fully grasp the meaning and magnitude of the data through exploratory analysis without effective visualization tools and experience at discerning between the noise (the Big Data) and the signal in the noise. Once you're comfortable with the noise, you can become adept at identifying the signal more readily. Getting comfortable with the noise is like immersing yourself in water.

Imagine that you're soaking in a bathtub. You can see and feel all the water surrounding you. The amount of water in the bathtub is like data sizes of the past that were within the grasp of a human mind to easily understand, digest, and synthesize. Now suppose that you add some Epsom salt to the water. The Epsom salt changes the chemistry in the water but doesn't visibly alter the bathtub water. In this analogy, is the water noise or signal? It's background noise. Is the Epsom salt a signal or noise? It is a signal for that particular bathtub since it is saturating the entire data set. That was a pretty clear signal but signals can be more subtle and harder to identify.

Now let's imagine a swimming pool, which is more comparable to today's typical production data sizes. It's a larger volume of water (chlorinated in this case) than the bathtub water but still within reasoning grasp. Now, as you're swimming through the pool, exploring the expanse of the pool, if you see a yellow streak from the shallow end of the pool where the kids are playing, you've just identified a continuous signal (and probably the source!). While this signal was a bit harder to find, it was strong and clear once you found it.

Now let's move to the North Atlantic Ocean. The ocean is comparable to tomorrow's data sizes that are so vast and expansive that you can't observe it all, yet you still need to in order to find the signal. Unfortunately, as you explore the North Atlantic, you'll notice nonbiodegradable trash occasionally littering the ocean. Depending on where you are in the North Atlantic, you may see occasional occurrences of trash or vast floating islands of it. The occasional observations of trash are discrete signals or short-lived continuous signals. These types of signals may be early warnings or may also be noise called *dirty data*. If you observe the data over time, you'll typically be able to determine if these types of data are emerging trends and therefore can be used as an early warning signal (see Figure 5.2).

Unfortunately, the mounds of floating trash islands are strong and clear signals of an accumulated trend. In the future, if we can identify trends early enough in the Big Data oceans, we can use that early warning signal to take early corrective actions and prevent the accumulation of signals that indicate we're in distress such as the floating islands of trash (see Figure 5.3).

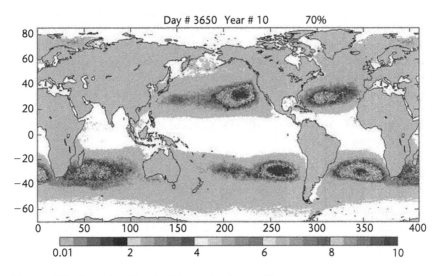

Figure 5.2 Emerging Signal of Ocean Trash over Time
Source: Ian Thomson, "Is the Ocean Safe from You and Your Boat?" MySailing.com, May 3, 2012, www.mysailing.com.au/news/is-the-ocean-safe-from-you-and-your-boat.

Figure 5.3 Potential Result of Ignoring Signals
Source: iStockphoto.com.

Finding signals can be like finding a needle in a haystack. The sheer data volume can cloud the signal or it could be that there is a long tail where a bulk of the signal is in the large area in the curve but the emerging signal is in the smallest area. Signals can also be cyclical and only emerge when viewed over a long period of time. Many economic cycles take 10 years to unfold. So, if you're only looking at three years of data you won't see the signal or may misinterpret the signal. Some signals are complex and require an understanding of several related factors to identify the signal. That's where the Big Data visualization tools are coming into play to make it easier to wrap your arms around the unwieldy data.

Consumption of Analytics

The Communication Cycle introduced in Chapter 6 (see Figure 6.4) provides a framework and process for making analytics consumable throughout an organization. Each of the stages in the cycle is key to enterprise synthesis of the analytics. Let's take a closer look at each of these stages:

- **Communication.** Successful consumption of analytics is a collaborative endeavor. The first step in this process is to take your analytics intent beyond your core team and sell it to a wider group of decision makers—the prospective daily consumers of analytics in your organization. The current economic scenario gives you a compelling storyline and helps you create a convincing platform to evangelize analytics in your organization.

- **Implement.** Organizations that successfully consume analytics are driven by leadership, which builds consensus in the organization and allows for moving ahead without the need to have everyone on board every step of the way. Strong leadership has been found to be the most important trigger in the wider analytics adoption in organizations. The initial focus of implementation should be on getting all the right ingredients in place to create the basic human and technology infrastructures to help you pluck the low hanging fruit.

- **Measure.** The true test of consumption is to use analytics to measure itself. However, the benefits need not always be translated in hard numbers. One often unanticipated but profound change in organizations is the maturing of a culture of objective debates, arguments, and viewpoints driven by data and not just "gut feel." Be forewarned against overestimating the impact of analytics by discounting the human element in it. A successful business decision is a healthy combination of business experience and analytics—both merit equal credit for successful analytics consumption.

- **Align incentives.** Successful consumption of analytics mandates creation of more structured decision-making processes, which is driven by data and analysis. This puts constraints on free-flowing, experience-driven decision making. The implementation will also bring in new stakeholders in your employees' decisions as well as higher levels of oversight. Sometimes a general tendency of status quo bias exists, and employees do not want to venture out of their comfort zone. You need to create robust incentives to overcome these barriers. However, creating well-aligned incentives is just one piece of the puzzle and is not fully sufficient to overcome this bias.

- **Develop cognitive repairs.** Our everyday decision making is influenced by numerous biases intrinsic to human nature. Presence of data and analysis challenges these biases and drives us out of our comfort zones. This results in undesirable conflicts and dysfunctional behaviors. The onus is on top leadership to make the decision makers in the organization aware of the presence of these biases. Creation of counterintuitive business insights based on data and then going and proving it right for all to see is by far the most effective to both expose biases and create repairs.

From Creation to Consumption

Various organizations in services as well as product-based industries have flawlessly executed on creating analytics but have failed miserably on consumption. Creating analytics does not automatically result in institutionalizing analytics. Whether or not your organization suffers from this challenge will be determined by your answers to these key questions:

- Do you have experience in creating a lot of analytics but failing at consumption?
- Does it make sense to ramp up/down analytics creation to maintain balance with consumption?
- Human bias exists. Do you need to develop structures that push people toward healthy conflict and resolution?

If the answer to any of these questions is affirmative, then your organization suffers from the creation-consumption gap. To put it another way, it is the difference between doing analytics and being analytical. While doing analytics focuses on creating analytics, being analytical balances and integrates creation of analytics with consumption of analytics. Organizations able to bridge this creation-consumption gap will be able to capitalize on analytics as a source of competitive advantage. Indeed, a key challenge that companies face is:

How to convert thought into action and bridge the gap between analytics creation and consumption?

Visualizing: How to Make It Consumable?

Visualizing data is a technique to facilitate the identification of patterns in data and presenting data to make it more consumable. Charts, graphs, and dashboards have been used for decades to synthesize data into a cohesive and comprehensible format for business analysts, managers, and executives. These techniques have been used to differentiate the contexts and intents of the data to be visualized. Intents such as:

- **Describing.** Attempting to explain the thing being described, for basic meaning
- **Reporting.** Summarizing findings from the past as of a point-in-time

However, as we move into the next stage of visualization, we move beyond these initial intents into the realm of:

- **Observing.** Viewing data to identify significance or patterns which unfold over a period of time
- **Discovering.** Interacting with data to explore, interact, and understand relationships between data

The need to differentiate these intents was inspired by Guido Stompff, a Senior Product Designer at Oce in the Netherlands. "Static visualizations are great to persuade, convince, and explain," he says, "but they also lack the feedback of change (time, impetus, etc.) and they often synthesize out the detail that might be needed for assessing cause and effect." Stompff suggests that visualization provides the ability to mitigate ambiguity, but he also sees challenges in doing so in situations that are themselves ambiguous. This is where "visualization in the raw" (thinking out loud) can be used to support a dialog: "Rather than visualizing what team members agree on," says Strompff, "the process of visualizing enables the dialogue, shows that people disagree and why." By allowing participants to "see" the words being spoken from another perspective, in a different form of abstraction, shared meaning emerges.

Describing and reporting intents have worked well for the current volume of information (the bathtub of water) but start to fail when data expands (the Atlantic Ocean). Seeing billions of points of data on a chart, graph, or dashboard simply doesn't accomplish the goal of helping to identify patterns. It makes the data overwhelming.

New techniques and tools are emerging that utilize exciting new visualizations and animations to visually depict *a story* about data that far exceeds the standard charts, graphs, and dashboards. An evolving term, *data artisans*, describes people who create these new and dynamic visualizations. Data artists are individuals with skills at the intersection of science, design, and art.

Aqumin CEO, Michael Zeitlin, formed his own company to specifically address the challenges of visualizing financial data. He notes that it's one thing to represent something tangible, such as geophysical data, but it's an entirely different challenge to figure out how to represent abstractions, like finance. "When you go to look at numbers," he says to explain the significance of visualization in cognition, "your brain has to convert them into patterns anyway."

Aqumin leverages relative size and color to help create comparative projections of data. Tapping the metaphor of a landscape, Figure 5.4 shows a

Figure 5.4   Big Data Landscape Visualization
Source: "AlphaVision Solutions—Marketplace Surveillance," Aqumin, July 10, 2012, https://aqumin.fogbugz.com/default.asp?W44.

series of "buildings" that represent market activity: the taller the building, the more "exceptions" that might represent questionable trading activity. This time series shows activity from market open to market close (lower left to upper right) for a number of market players (sequence of rows). There are a total of 16,000 data points shown in this image. Intended for use by financial regulators, each data point is accessible in real time for "drill down" (i.e., getting more information). Prior to this technology, tracking data this way was impossible. Representing both tangible and intangible things visually includes infinitely greater possibilities at a far lower price point than even 10 years ago.

It's interesting to watch as the effort to create lifelike renderings from data (e.g., scientific, academic, business) converges with the output of data from life itself. Somewhere in the middle you will find Donna Cox, a research scientist and artist. Dr. Cox started her career in film and by 2010 you'd find her at TEDx events giving presentations on *visiphors*, or digital visual metaphors. These are powerful renderings of complex systems that make the previously unknowable explainable. Visiphors are created by mapping numbers into pictures; it is a term equally applied to a stand-alone animation or an interactive application.

As the field of visualization matures, data artisans are using many different dimensions to represent and/or evaluate data. A sampling of such dimensions and attributes include:

- Spatial, geospatial: position, direction, velocity
- Temporal, periodicity: state, cycle, phase
- Scale, granularity: weight, size, count
- Relativity, proximity
- Value, priority
- Resources: energy, temperature, matter
- Constraints

A static visual representation can never address multiple dimensions effectively, nor can it effectively show change over time. A series of static representations can only approximate change through periodic snapshots.

But looking at and observing data through visualization, even complex animations, isn't the same as interacting with it to uncover deeper meaning. It requires an effort to traverse and explore the data to uncover these various dimensions. Dr. Cox suggests that such mechanisms assist in our ability to explore and engage in wayfaring for discovery, interpretation, and deeper understanding.

Jeffrey Heer and Ben Shneiderman expressed in their academic paper "Interactive Dynamics for Visual Analysis":

The increasing scale and availability of digital data provides an extraordinary resource for informing public policy, scientific discovery, business strategy, and even our personal lives. To get the most out of such data, however, users must be able to make sense of it: to pursue questions, uncover patterns of interest, and identify (and potentially correct) errors. In concert with data-management systems and statistical algorithms, analysis requires contextualized human judgments regarding the domain-specific significance of the clusters, trends, and outliers discovered in data.[1]

They reiterate the contribution of visualization to *sensemaking*:

Visualization provides a powerful means of making sense of data. By mapping data attributes to visual properties such as position, size, shape, and color, visualization designers leverage perceptual skills to help users discern and interpret patterns within data. A single image, however, typically provides answers to, at best, a handful of questions. Instead, visual analysis typically progresses in an iterative process of view creation, exploration, and refinement. Meaningful analysis consists of repeated explorations as users develop insights about significant relationships, domain-specific contextual influences, and causal patterns.[2]

The authors raise several important points worth reiterating. One, they identify a distinct role of *visualization designer* and two, they note the nonstatic nature of the topic: "visual analysis typically progresses in an iterative process of view creation, exploration, and refinement." Last, they indirectly suggest that because of what is learned over time and in different contexts that this could/should be a social activity.

In 1998, Robert M. Edsall, Mark Harrower, and Jeremy L. Mennis insisted that both the images and the interactivity are fundamental to the definition of visualization:

Visualization refers not only to a set of graphical images but also to the iterative process of visual thinking and interaction with the images. An interactive visualization environment, in which the user may choose to display the data in many different ways, encourages data exploration. One goal of data exploration is the recognition of pattern and the abstraction of structure and meaning from data. Interactivity is a necessary complement to animation; enabling users to control the pace, direction, and selection of frames of an animated display is vital for the most complete understanding of the data. Interactivity is thus a basic need for flexible user-centered visualization.[3]

As the *New York Times* data artist in residence, Jer Thorp suggests in his 2012 TEDxVancouver presentation "The Weight of Data" that we need to traverse the data and leverage it as an exploratory tool. He notes that visualization helps us build narrative structures to describe the history—what happened. Beyond that, we have to explore in other ways, why it happened.

Another example of issues with visualization was offered by Creve Maples, author of "Beyond Visualization—Productivity, Complexity and Information Overload," at the O'Reilly Strata Conference in February 2011. It's relevant to note that Dr. Maples acquired his own visualization skills (including developing visualization tools) through his work as a nuclear physicist—attempting to understand complex, multidimensional data. For his Strata presentation in Santa Clara, California, he took the data set of all the conference talk abstracts and let a clustering tool create a word cloud of relevant terms. While the tool insisted that it was removing "common words," he pointed out that it didn't know enough about the context of the conference to know the many terms that should be common in this case, such as *session, talk, present, inc*, and the

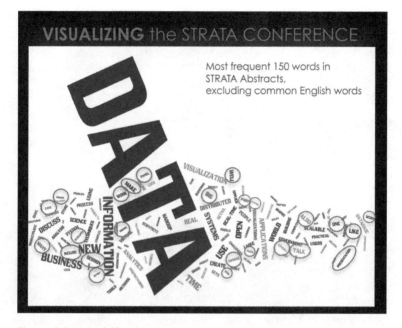

Figure 5.5   Word Cloud
Source: Creve Maples, "Beyond Visualization—Productivity, Complexity and Information Overload," O'Reilly Strata Conference, Event Horizon Corporation, Santa Clara, California, February 3, 2011.

like. These words effectively become "noise" in the visual output. It requires some intervention to make the output useful to support a compelling and meaningful story.

In Figure 5.5, the weighted representation of "information" (left of "data") appears to be almost twice as big as "visualization" (upper right of "data"). Yet in a reworked version (see Figure 5.6) they appear to be almost equal. This is a highly simplified example of how tools can distort meaning.

Creve pointed out that someone might draw the wrong conclusions about the conference if they judged it purely based on this representation. He more specifically noted that the real purpose of visualization is to provide "insight and understanding" and yet these terms are barely visible. He also circled back to reiterate that "data is passive" and "information is active." Visualization is a means by which to put data in a relevant context so that it can "inform." He added, "When we focus on data itself we somehow forget its meaning." The challenge is to avoid misinforming the recipient.

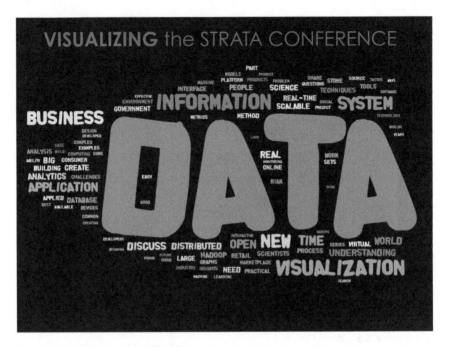

Figure 5.6   Revised Word Cloud
Source: Creve Maples, "Beyond Visualization—Productivity, Complexity and Information Overload," O'Reilly Strata Conference, Event Horizon Corporation, Santa Clara, California, February 3, 2011.

Interactive data visualization and discovery tools, such as Tableau, are shifting insight discovery from a handful of specialists to everyone in the business. Ravi Bandaru, Nokia's Product Manager for Advanced Data Visualizations and Data Analytics, has been using Tableau since July 2010. Within his organization, he said about 350 to 400 people use Tableau—either in desktop or interactive form—and that it has brought people together. "It's letting the analyst do more analysis himself or herself without IT coming between them and their data," he said. "Using this kind of in-memory capability, I do see this being useful in exploring more complex and largish data sets, which were inaccessible before."

Organizations Are Using Data Visualization as a Way to Take Immediate Action

Interactive data visualization is another way to change the typical iterative or cycle times of Big Data analytics so that insights can be made actionable.

Take Playdom, which is a leading social gaming company with millions of users. The company collects massive amounts of data—about a billion rows a day—and uses Tableau for analytics and reporting. Product managers analyze tables of hundreds of millions of rows interactively to understand user dynamics or problems in their games. Vice President of Analytics, David Botkin, describes the impact that fast queries have on their business: "The difference is hundreds of iterations. It means we can ask questions, ask follow up questions, cut the data in many different ways . . . That's just the right way to do analysis." With Tableau, Playdom's people have the freedom to ask and answer questions visually and in real time, instead of waiting hours to get query results. Tableau gives Playdom "the ability to rapidly understand the behavior of our customers on our games and to figure out what's working for them and what's not."

We spoke with advanced analytics guru Chuck Alvarez from Morgan Stanley, who used the analogy of the human nervous system to describe the use of visualization to relay messages:

I like to use the analogy of the central nervous system and the brain is part of the central nervous system. You've got a brain which tells you what to do, when to do it. The brain collects history about past events. The brain deduces things. The brain induces things. The brain talks to muscles through the nervous system, of which there are multiple nervous systems—some are involuntary, some voluntary—but you get the picture. You take the analogy of an organization. An organization has a brain. An organization has a nervous system. An organization has muscle. All these things provide an organization to move, to ultimately become profitable.

If you take a look at it and draw your standard layered model you have information events and facts about those events. Your intellect as your analytics and your nervous system is your distribution. You need to have all the core skills embodied in the data scientist that reside in a number of individuals. There are the obvious skills needed such as a high level of intelligence, math skills, and technical knowledge. There is one indistinct but critical skill that relays messages back and forth from the brain to different parts of the body (your organization); an understanding of how to induce/deduce and deliver insight that is actionable.

In order to be successful your team needs to communicate as part of the central nervous system that feeds business decisions. The story is not complete without a way to be able to push insight that can be interpreted by the business and followed up with action. That's data visualization and I am a huge fan of that.

Fundamentally, when I say making these things actionable, action is about execution. In order to be successful, it comes down to having the right data analytics talent, great data visualization, and a process that enables the execution."

Big Data visualization is still in the early stages and there are a few commercial vendors that are leading the charge along with a wide variety of open-source projects. Here are some examples of the currently available tools and open-source projects:

- Tableau, www.tableausoftware.com
- Qlikview, www.qlikview.com
- Microstrategy, www.microstrategy.com
- D3JS, Data Driven Documents java script library, http://d3js.org
- SAS, www.sas.com
- Gephi Org, open-source data visualization platform, https://gephi.org
- Flowing Data, a community for data artists to understand and share visualization techniques, http://flowingdata.com
- Arbor JS, a Java-based graph library, http://arborjs.org
- Cubism, a plug-in for D3 for visualizing time series, http://square.github.com/cubism
- GeoCommons, a community building an open mapping platform, http://geocommons.com
- JavaScript InfoVis Toolkit, http://thejit.org
- ManyEyes, data visualization tools from IBM Research, http://www-958.ibm.com/software/data/cognos/manyeyes

Let's take a look at various Big Data visualizations that are emerging today. Figure 5.7 is a typical interactive dashboard where the business user can easily see various analytics in the context of their business and can drill down easily.

Within Figure 5.7, there is a simple example of powerful visualization that the Tableau team is referring to. A company uses an interactive dashboard to track the critical metrics driving their business. Every day, the CEO and other executives are plugged in real-time to see how their markets are performing in terms of sales and profit, what the service quality scores look like against advertising investments, and how products are performing in terms of revenue and profit. Interactivity is key: a click on any filter lets the executive look into specific markets or products. She can click on any data point in any one view to show the related data in the other views. Hovering over a data point lets her winnow into any unusual pattern or outlier by

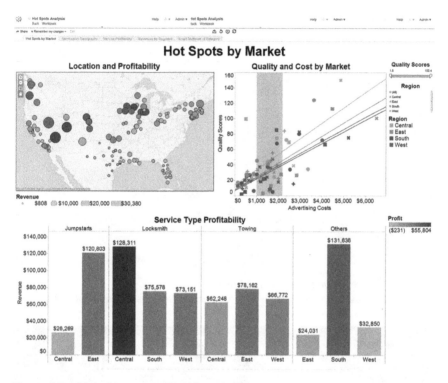

Figure 5.7 Typical Interactive Dashboard
Source: Visualization example from Tableau Software, www.tableau.com.

showing details on demand. Or she can click through the underlying information in a split-second.

This next visualization (see Figure 5.8) is an interactive visualization that shows the location of a bus in real time in a busy commuter city, Sydney. Each city bus has a GPS and is sending location information in real time and that location information is being used to determine the optimal routes.

Visualizing data over time is a particularly difficult challenge and there are very interesting visualizations that are evolving to illustrate Big Data over time. Figure 5.9 is a global climate change visualization that shows temperatures around the world over the last 200 years.

Another style of illustrating data over time is an interactive flow visualization as illustrated at http://hint.fm/wind/. This visualization depicts the surface wind flows in the United States over the last 200 years.

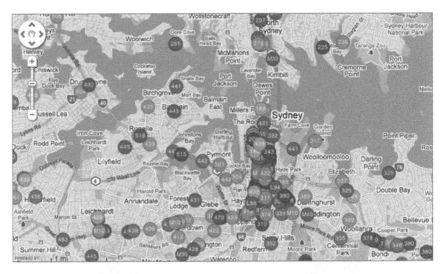

Figure 5.8 Interactive Location Visualization
Source: "FLINKLABS Our Work," July 10, 2012, www.flinklabs.com/portfolio.php.

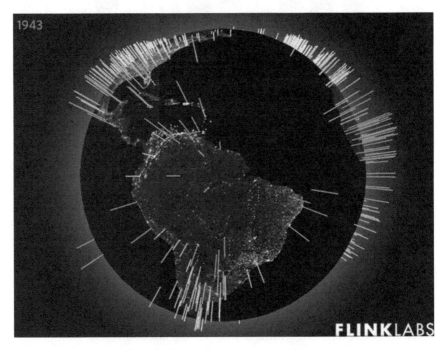

Figure 5.9 Visualization of Temperature Trends Globally
Source: "FLINKLABS Our Work," July 10, 2012, www.flinklabs.com/portfolio.php.

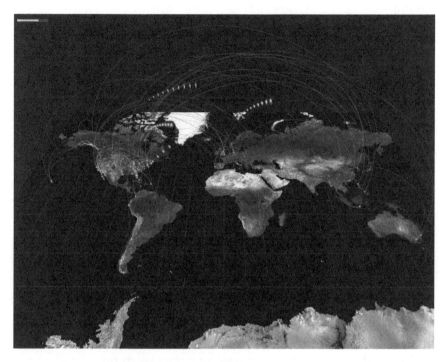

Figure 5.10 Twitter Propagation across the Globe
Source: JerThorp@blog.blprnt.com, "The Weight of Data," TEDxVancouver, July 10, 2012, www.youtube.com/watch?v=Q9wcvFkWpsM.

This next visualization, Figure 5.10, combines two very difficult perspectives, time and geography, to illustrate the origin and propagation of Twitter messages around the globe.

Moving from Sampling to Using All the Data

Traditionally, models have been created using a subset of the data called a *sample*. Once the model was created, a second larger set of data was used to test or validate the model. This process was often iterative. Once the model was validated, the model was used to evaluate or "score" all the data. This is a well-known statistical approach that has been used for decades. With Big Data, data scientists are using more or all of the data to create the model. By doing this, data scientists are able to introduce additional predictor variables into the model in order to increase the lift (accuracy) of the model. When more historical Big Data is used, the model can identify trends that are outside of the truncated cycles that were used in the historical data extraction technique. For example, in the financial services industry, due to data and computational limits, market models were created with a relatively short period of time (i.e., three to five years) but many of the economic cycles unfold over a 10-year period. Big Data affords data scientists in the financial industry the opportunity to create models over the required time horizon.

Thinking Outside the Box

As multidisciplinary thinkers, data scientists are using multiple techniques to create analytic models to meet business objectives. For example, data scientists are using more "ensemble models," which unite multiple models taking the best of each model to generate the best predictive results. (For more information, read Giovanni Seni and John Elder, "Ensemble Methods in Data Mining: Improving Accuracy Through Combining Predictions."[4]) Other data scientists are chaining together techniques to generate the best results. For example, data scientists create a predictive model using well-known algorithmic techniques then use simulation techniques to evaluate millions of scenarios and then apply optimization techniques to maximize the model output. By thinking outside the box about the approach, data scientists are able to generate better results for their enterprise.

360° Modeling

Today, models that are deployed into production environments are periodically reevaluated by their creators. The frequency by which models are reevaluated varies tremendously. As Big Data environments unfold, businesses are demanding that models are continuously reevaluated to obtain additional lift from the models as the data evolves over time. This can be done by creating a closed loop, where learnings are manually incorporated by the data scientist and/or machine learning techniques can be employed that learn and adapt based on the new data.

Need for Speed

In eras gone by, enterprises moved from manual processes to automated processes to gain efficiencies. As analytics initially evolved, much of the analytics processing was performed as special ad hoc projects or in offline batch processes.

In today's hyperconnected world, enterprises are trying to "pulse" faster and faster to stay ahead of the competition. Enterprises trying to keep this grueling pace are moving to near-real-time processing where the data is analyzed as quickly as it is consumed. Big Data technologies enable faster pulsing since there's much less of a delay in getting data and turning the data into insights. This allows an organization to predict next likely moves or to take corrective action much faster.

For example, while a consumer is shopping on a website for a new innovative camera, the clicks and actions taken on the website can be used to create personalized offers to drive additional revenues such as a warranty, an additional battery, and a carrying case. While these are the "obvious" recommendations, additional unrelated recommendations, such as a prepurchase of the to-be released iPad and iPhone or apps for photo editing, could also be made based on the buyer's likely profile (e.g., high-disposable-income gadget buyer).

An example of early corrective actions can occur when the sensors on your car send information to the automotive manufacturer, and the manufacturer uses the information to anticipate issues with the car and alert the driver that the car needs to be serviced, or the customer care center calls the driver to personally alert the driver to a potentially dangerous situation.

Let's Get Scrappy

Today, we have a mountain of enterprise problems to solve and finally have the data and computational power to solve them. The increased revenue and cost-savings potential are significant enough to power a decade of economic growth. So rather than spending time building new algorithmic techniques, we need to harness our best and brightest minds on "getting scrappy" to solve real-world problems with Big Data analytics. While bright minds that thrive on innovation and recognition might initially be turned off by this proposition, we should focus them on the recognition of accomplishing something tangible. It's like when I need my car cleaned. I can pay someone to clean it (which I do sometimes) but I feel so much better when I clean it myself. The fruits of my labor are visible and tangible. The innovation in this era is in *applying* all of these well-known and developed algorithmic techniques into analytic models. Leave the algorithmic development to those working in or for industries such as financial services or digital media companies that are very mature and seasoned in applying analytics on big data. In these matured industries, the focus should be on inventing a new algorithmic technique with seemingly minor incremental technical benefits that can result in gargantuan economic benefit.

What Technology Is Available?

All the traditional players such as SAS, IBM SPSS, KXEN, Matlab, Statsoft, Tableau, Pentaho, and others are working toward Hadoop-based Big Data analytics. However, each of these software players has to balance their current technology and customer portfolio along with the incredulous pace of innovation occurring in the open-source community. Most of the tools have connectors that are high-speed connectors to move data back and forth between Hadoop and their tool/environment. With Big Data, the objective is to keep the data in place and bring the analytics processing to the data to avoid the bottleneck and constraints associated with data movement. Over time, each vendor will develop a strategy and approach to keep data in place and move their analytics processing to the data.

In the meantime, there are new commercial vendors and open-source projects evolving to address the voracious appetite for Big Data analytics. Karmasphere (https://karmasphere.com/) is a native Hadoop-based tool for data exploration and visualization. Datameer (http://www.datameer.com/) is a spreadsheet-like presentation tool. Alpine Data Miner (http://www.alpinedatalabs.com/) has a cross-platform analytic workbench.

R (http://cran.r-project.org/) is by far the most dominant analytics tool in the Big Data space. R is an open-source statistical language with constructs that make it easy for data scientists to explore and build models. R is also renowned for the plethora of available analytics. There are libraries focused on industry problems (i.e., clinical trials, genetics, finance, and others) as well as general purpose libraries (i.e., econometrics, natural language processing, optimization, time series, and many more). At this point, there are supposedly over two million R users around the globe and a commercial distribution is available via Revolution Analytics.

Open-source technologies include:

- Apache Mahout, a scalable, Hadoop machine learning library, http://mahout.apache.org
- Apache Lucene, a high-performance text search library, http://lucene.apache.org/core
- Sofia ML, a fast machine learning library, http://code.google.com/p/sofia-ml
- Vowpal Wabbit, a Yahoo! Research project for fast, parallel-learning algorithms, http://hunch.net/~vw
- Libocas, a library of support vector machine solvers, http://cmp.felk.cvut.cz/~xfrancv/ocas/html

- Apache Hamster, an MPI for Hadoop, https://issues.apache.org/jira/browse/MAPREDUCE-2911
- Julia, a high-performance, parallel distribution analytics language for analytics computing, http://julialang.org/

Moving from Beyond the Tools to Analytic Applications

Big Data platforms and tools are the current state of affairs. However, it's clear that none of these make it easy for a business to achieve the promise of Big Data. In order to fully capitalize on the Big Data value, Big Data apps are starting to emerge. Both horizontal Big Data Apps (e.g., machine log analytics by Splunk, http://www.splunk.com/) and vertical Big Data apps (e.g., telecommunications analytics by Guavus, http://www.guavus.com/) are emerging. Big Data apps are designed to address specific business problems and incorporate deeper, more complex prescriptive analytics typically while also allowing the power business analysts the ability to explore the data. This allows organizations to more readily deploy a solution and to achieve the 100X to 500X ROI that organizations are achieving with their Big Data analytics.

At the end of the day, Big Data analytics is about pulsing faster. Just as the trading world has forever been changed by algorithmic trading where buys and sells are done automatically without human intervention based on complex algorithms and decisions, the rest of the business world is about to be disrupted with other frictionless decisions that will effectively cause businesses to pulse faster. And in this new era, he who pulses faster wins.

Notes

1. Jeffrey Heer and Ben Shneiderman, "Interactive Dynamics for Visual Analysis," February 12, 2012, ACM Queue, http://queue.acm.org/detail.cfm?id=2146416.
2. Ibid.
3. Robert M Edsall, Mark Harrower, and Jeremy L. Mennis, "Tools for Visualizing Properties of Spatial and Temporal Periodicity in Geographic Data," *Computers & Geosciences* 26 (2000): 109–118, http://astro.temple.edu/~jmennis/pubs/mennis_cg00.pdf.
4. Giovanni Seni, John Elder, and Robert Grossman, "Ensemble Methods in Data Mining: Improving Accuracy through Combining Predictions," Morgan and Claypool Publishers, February 24, 2010, www.morganclaypool.com/doi/pdf/10.2200/S00240ED1V01Y200912DMK002.

CHAPTER 6

The People Part of the Equation

In the end, it all comes down to people. The best of intentions can go awry if the goals of the analytics professionals and the end business consumers are not aligned. This is even more critical given the highly iterative nature of analytics, which demands that generators and consumers work closely on a continuous basis. The three major activities that must occur to ensure success are:

1. **Organizational alignment.** The leaders need to define business priorities and problems to be solved and define road maps that are time-bound but at the same time measurable and achievable. As intuitive as it may seem, without focus and direction, no processes or technology will make a difference.
2. **Executive endorsement and sponsorship.** It is important for the leadership team to endorse fact-based decision making and identify champions for consumption of analytics. Consumption also requires a lot of walking the aisles, socializing the insights, and maneuvering the dynamics across various business groups. Without conscious focus on these activities, the visually rich reports or sophisticated statistical models will not drive any real business value.
3. **Investing in analytical human capital.** The organization needs to mobilize resources required for analytics and hire the right talent and retain them. There is an increasing demand for analysts who can learn new skills as the situation demands, be it math, business, or technology.

In today's business world, every single business function is questioning the need for analytics. Yet, as it often happens in an evolving discipline, companies that are investing in analytics often find that the businesses do not consume the outputs for a variety of reasons. As companies realize that one of the many factors that separate failure from success is their ability to effectively use analytics to make better decisions, it becomes necessary for the key stakeholders to ensure the right set of investments are made on the process, technology, and people dimensions to bridge the gap between the creation and consumption of analytics. The sooner businesses can get this done, the better their chances are of leveraging the potential competitive advantage offered by analytics.

Speaking of analytic talent, there is a *major* shortage. According to a McKinsey study, there will be approximately 140,000 to 190,000 unfilled positions of data analytics experts in the United States by 2018 and a shortage of 1.5 million managers and analysts who have the ability to understand and make decisions using Big Data.

If you have a child, friend, or relative who likes math, problem solving, or has creativity for data visualization be sure to steer them toward the world of analytics. It's not only an edge; in most cases, it's a guaranteed way to get a job after college.

Rise of the Data Scientist

Every trend generates a countertrend, and the field of data analytics isn't immune to this phenomenon. For a number of years, the field has been steadily democratized by the astonishingly rapid emergence of exciting new tools and technologies for crunching through increasingly large mountains of data. The availability of all this "new gear" has made some aspects of data analysis seem easier or, at least, less daunting. And there lies the problem. According to David Champagne, CTO of Revolution Analytics:

> Back in the good old days, data was the stuff generated by scientific experiments. Remember the scientific method? First you ask a question, then you construct a hypothesis, and then you design an experiment. Then you run your experiment, collect the data, analyze the data, and draw conclusions. Then you communicate your results and let other people throw rocks at them. Nowadays, thanks largely to all of the newer tools and techniques available for handling larger and larger sets of data, we often start with the data. Then we build models around the data, run the models, and see what happens.

This is less like science and more like panning for gold. Several data analysts interviewed for this book describe the current trend as "throwing spaghetti against the wall and seeing what sticks." When you consider the paramount importance of data analytics in virtually every human endeavor (finance, health care, telecommunications, manufacturing, travel, government, etc.), the sticky spaghetti image seems particularly unappetizing.

Yesterday and Today

- *Business* + *Math* gave rise to the consulting profession. This allowed us to use heuristics and creativity to make persuasive arguments in the boardroom.
- *Business* + *Technology* gave rise to the IT profession. This helped us automate algorithmic tasks, thus improving productivity and efficiency.
- *Math* + *Technology* inspired interesting software products that helped us address a wide range of business problems and operate proactively with anticipation.

Tomorrow

- *Business* + *Math* + *Technology* are coming together with the behavioral sciences. The behavioral sciences allow us to connect the dots between interactions and develop a deeper understanding of human behavior. Combining that deep understanding with math and technology allows us to create the appropriate incentives to drive behaviors that align to our business goals as illustrated in Figure 6.1.

Sustaining such a culture of decision sciences will need a combination of necessary traits:

- **Inferential learning over experiential knowledge.** Ability to apply first principles and structured approaches to problem solving

Figure 6.1 Evolution of Data Science

as opposed to relying excessively on past domain expertise. Since business is transforming rapidly it is no longer relevant to what one knew five years back; it is more important to be able to infer and learn from what happened in the past few months, weeks, days, and so on.

- **Agility.** Needed to cope with continuous transformation. Organizations will need to design their organizations to be agile from all three perspectives: people, process, and technology. This implies adopting agile frameworks that enable fast iterations, front-loaded thinking, hypothesis, and visualization.
- **Scale and convergence.** Synergistic ecosystem of talent, capabilities, processes, customers, and partners that can be leveraged across verticals, domains, and geographies.
- **Multi-disciplinary talent.** Ability to apply Business + Math + Technology + Behavioral Sciences.
- **Innovation.** Increase breadth and depth of problem solving by constantly researching and deploying emerging techniques, technologies, and applications.
- **Cost effectiveness.** Ensure sustainability and institutionalization of problem solving across organizations.

Learning over Knowing

Learning and knowing are two completely different things. Learning comes with experience and is associated with taking risks. Knowing is more about prior knowledge (i.e., "gut feeling") or, perhaps, the result of being "told" that a certain fact is true without questioning it. It is the converse of learning and often not based on fact.

One does not need a Ph.D., formal training in statistics, or proficiency in programming logic to get started on decision sciences. It is possible for analysts with, as I mentioned, a good hypothesis-driven mind-set, basic statistical knowledge, good database skills, and a keen understanding of the business and its underlying data to create effective models using spreadsheets. Understanding the information available, applying it in the right context, and asking the right set of questions are the keys to successfully practicing decision sciences. To quote a famous statistician, John Tukey, "An approximate answer to the right problem is worth a great deal more than an exact answer to an approximate problem." It is equally important that decision sciences are embedded into business processes, to improve the ability of the organization to discover new actionable insights and reduce the gap between insights, decisions, and actions.

Agility

Today more than ever, we live in a rapidly changing, hypercompetitive, disruptive world. In such a world, agility in making decisions becomes very critical. One cannot wait for weeks to understand the performance of a campaign or understand customer behavior. Organizations will have to engage in information arbitrage games to exploit information asymmetry with the competition. Specifically, in analytically mature industry sectors, information advantage would be a swiftly moving target due to the intense competition.

In such an environment, to enable businesses to make data-driven decisions, decision sciences professions need to adopt agility as a key value and need to cope with continuous transformation in their thinking and in actions.

Scale and Convergence

With the blurring of value chain boundaries and the emergence of new business models, a new era of convergence in the use of techniques and frameworks will come into play. Cross-industry and cross-domain learning will lead to significant breakthroughs in the development and deployment of analytics solutions.

Application of new business models in existing companies is accelerating the need for convergence and collaboration, such as Microsoft entering retail, cellular phone network providers entering the netbook category, Dell moving from custom configurations to pre-built offerings, and so on.

Scottrade and Yahoo! are collaborating on data and analytics to optimize lead generation for Scottrade. Historically, certain analytical techniques have been developed and utilized mostly in specific domains. For example, yield optimization in airlines, survival modeling in life sciences, lean principles in manufacturing, diversification in finance, and so forth. However, these techniques have a strong potential to be used across industries, such as yield optimization methodologies for the online advertising industry, survival modeling concepts for financial risk analytics, and diversification for marketing and supply chains.

The ability to learn from multiple industries and leverage cross-domain learning is a key trait needed to excel as a decision science professional.

Multidisciplinary Talent

While analytics helps us gain insights and make decisions, those decisions can create a positive impact only if human biases are taken into account during implementation. Analytics-based insights will challenge many traditional ways of working. Professionals trying to champion data-driven decision making will need to leverage an interdisciplinary approach using

Business + Technology + Mathematics + Behavioral Economics + Social Anthropology. As this becomes a formal practice in corporate operating procedures and corporate strategies, better understanding of human biases would help develop cognitive repairs or nudges to ensure better application of decisions.

Today, more and more organizations are investing in dedicated consumer insights teams. They focus on developing segmentation strategies, understanding customer lifetime value, market sizing, and so on as independent initiatives. Over the next few years, they will move toward a holistic approach to understand their customers.

Innovation

The use of decision sciences will enable companies to leverage continuous innovation.

Typically, the speed of innovation is inversely proportional to the kind of innovation. Disruptive innovations tend to take longer to release and have a longer shelf life. Incremental innovations tend to be faster to create and can be relatively easier to replicate.

Many companies invest in incremental innovation strategies using the investments they have made in their data assets. At the same time, the true disruptive innovators would focus on creating the right mix of qualitative and quantitative analytics by bringing in new areas such as behavioral economics and social anthropology to create and execute innovative ideas.

The drive to innovate by constantly researching and deploying emerging techniques, technologies, applications, and learnings from solving a variety of business problems is important for any decision sciences profession, in order to see their work get consumed and lead to high-impact decisions.

Cost Effectiveness

Any idea or concept that needs large-scale adoption needs to be cost effective. For example, if the cost of a personal computer didn't come down to a level that was acceptable to a large population, it would never have become a household item.

The mobile phone was originally a fashion statement for celebrities and television shows during its debut. It was only when the technology became cheaper that the public began to buy the new emerging models.

Similarly, if data-driven decision making needs to be adopted at a large scale, it needs to be cost effective. The cost of an analysis should not be too high from a time, effort, people, and process perspective. Organizations and professionals in the decision sciences industry need to strive to be cost effective to make decision sciences commonplace.

Using Deep Math, Science, and Computer Science

Big Data by itself is simply a nightmare. It's hard to create, manage, and make heads or tails of. So why is everyone so enamored with Big Data? It's because of the potential game-changing value that can be derived from the Big Data. That promise is why enterprises worldwide, big and small, across every industry are trying to figure out how to capitalize on the Big Data potential. If Big Data was a human body, Big Data analytics would be the heart, the Big Data would be the nervous system bringing blood to and out of the heart, and Big Data visualization would be the exterior of the body that makes you interested in engaging with the person. Each piece of the Big Data body is important and key to attaining the end result and the heart is at the center of creating the value.

Data scientists are the resources on the team who create that value by combining their deep math, science, and computer science backgrounds to address specific business problems. With their deep expertise, data scientists can quickly learn the industry or business and apply their knowledge to solving tough business problems. If you have a data scientist with deep domain/industry background they are extraordinarily valuable because they can more quickly resolve problems and can anticipate issues that haven't been identified yet.

Data scientists are naturally curious. They tend to probe and investigate problems and curiosities that other busy businesspeople tend to discount or ignore. For example, a data scientist tends to be curious about anomalies and infrequent occurrences in order to determine if those are emerging trends (i.e., longer cycle trends) or outliers (i.e., long-tail evaluation). In a nutshell, data scientists investigate data to determine the relation of the data and the data patterns to determine the impact on the outcomes.

Data scientists use their natural curiosity, math, science, computer science, and domain knowledge skills to create models that are representations of the data and patterns. These models are used to predict future outcomes based on patterns from past data. Data scientists are adept at experimenting and often use simulation techniques to evaluating multiple scenarios (i.e., "what if" scenarios based on a variety of potential starting or changed conditions). In addition to using models for predicting and simulating, models can be used to optimize for particular goal(s). The results of optimization are specific prescriptive actions to take in order to achieve the goal(s). For example, optimization has been utilized in supply chains to reduce costs and streamline operations, and financial analysis has been used to optimize portfolios for target yields. Optimization techniques are very mathematically intensive and, with Big Data, the computation requirements become massive. The experienced data scientist is knowledgeable in a variety of scientific approaches, including optimization, which takes into account uncertainty (i.e., unforeseen events), complex interrelationships (i.e., impact of geopolitical events on competitive market pressures), and conflicting multiobjectives (i.e., maximize revenue and market share while minimizing marketing budget spend and slowly growing international sales).

Data scientists have a breadth of skills and knowledge that are difficult to find. Data scientists typically have a Ph.D. or Master's degree, which means that you're not going to simply "train up" a team easily. The good news is that you can surround your top data scientists with other top resources to increase their productivity. For example, experienced database developers and data miners have complementary skills that can work very effectively in a team with the data scientist.

The countertrend is what Nathan Yau calls "the rise of the data scientist." Yau is a Ph.D. candidate at UCLA. His area of concentration is statistics with a focus in data visualization, and he writes a popular blog, *FlowingData*. From his perspective, really good data analysis is more than merely a matter of crunching numbers. It's a blend of talents and specialties. Here's a snippet from Yau's seminal post on the subject:

> Think about all the visualization stuff you've been most impressed with or the groups that always seem to put out the best work. Martin Wattenberg. Stamen Design. Jonathan Harris. Golan Levin. Sep Kamvar. Why is their work always of such high quality? Because they're not just students of computer science, math, statistics, or graphic design.
>
> They have a combination of skills that not just makes independent work easier and quicker; it makes collaboration more exciting and opens up possibilities in what can be done.

Yau's post, along with posts in a similar vein from other bloggers, has sparked an energetic conversation in the data analytics community. Not all data analysts are entirely comfortable with the idea of being called "data scientists." But there is an emerging sense of agreement that to be genuinely effective, a data analyst must bring more to the table than a keen ability to analyze data.

So at this point, it seems fair to ask, how are data scientists different from data analysts? Drew Conway, a former member of the intelligence community, and PhD graduate in political science from New York University, is now Scientist in Residence at IA Ventures. He recently posted a Venn diagram that depicts his vision of the overlapping skill sets required for data scientists (see Figure 6.2). In Conway's formulation, the major skill sets are:

1. Hacking skills
2. Math and statistical knowledge
3. Substantive expertise

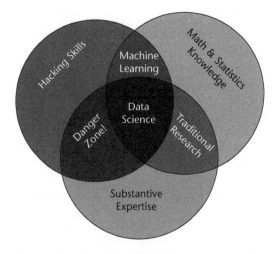

Figure 6.2   Data Scientist Skills
Source: Drew Conway.

As Conway sees it, a true data scientist must also be a "speak hacker." That certainly makes sense, since most data today exists as a sequence of ones and zeroes in a database. Data scientists don't have to be hard-core computer geeks, says Conway, but they do have to know their way around the IT landscape because that's where the data lives. Hacking abilities are important because data tends to reside in multiple locations, and in multiple systems. Finding and retrieving data sometimes requires the skills of a burglar—even when the data is in the public domain, owned by your organization, or owned by another organization that has agreed to let you use it.

The Venn diagram is useful, but it is important to highlight that one person can't do all of this. This is why many companies strive to create teams that work as one to cover all of the bases.

Perhaps the term "data scientist" reflects a desire to see data analysis return to its scientific roots. "I'm not a big fan of the spaghetti method," says Zubin Dowlaty, Vice President of Innovation and Development at Mu Sigma, a global analytics services company. "It makes me nervous when people run a lot of analytic techniques just to get the answer they want, instead of being objective. Doing this job properly requires the rigor of a scientist. The scientist can see things that other people cannot see."

With or without a new moniker, the analytics industry is changing, says Dowlaty. "The trend is toward a multidisciplinary approach to extracting value from data. It's not just about math anymore. You also need technology skills. But what ultimately separates the analyst from the scientist is the dimension of artistic creativity. It's the soft skills that make the big difference."

Michael Driscoll, author of Dataspora Blog, holds a Ph.D. in Bioinformatics from Boston University and an A.B. from Harvard College. He has a decade of experience developing data platforms and predictive algorithms for telecom, financial, and life sciences institutions. From his perspective, the rise of data science represents the next logical phase of innovation in business intelligence.

"Think of it as a three-layer cake with data management at the bottom, BI software in the middle, and insights at the top," says Driscoll. "Data management is, increasingly, a solved problem. BI vendors could be facing a mass extinction. We're moving up the stack into the next phase, towards analytics, which drives products."

Whether you call it data analysis or data science, the future of this field looks brilliant *and* exciting.

The 90/10 Rule and Critical Thinking

Once again, we come back to our talks with Avinash Kaushik, Google's digital marketing evangelist, and the author of two best-selling books, *Web Analytics 2.0* and *Web Analytics: An Hour a Day*. At Google, he has a consumer-facing role and an inner-facing role. In the inner-facing role, he has to work with the core teams that provide consumer facing data and help influence the shape and direction of those tools. *Where should they go? What data will be more useful to consumers? What metrics should we think about and what kind of psychographic analysis should we think about next?* Externally, his role is twofold: work with CEOs/CMOs to help reshape their thinking about digital marketing.

A common theme in the Big Data space is definitely the huge shift in new and more cost-effective technology. However, there is an element that is one of the biggest assets for companies: people (Big Data analytics talent).

When Kaushik wrote his first book, he had developed a "10/90 rule" for technology and talent. After what he explains as his "painful failures in the digital world," he conceptually gave himself $100 to make smart decisions on the Web. He believes that the key to success is investing $10 in systems and invest $90 in the people who analyze the data.

In the digital marketing space, he believes that we will have systems and platforms that are going to become increasingly smarter so the tactical decisions will all be automated with real-time decisions that are handled without human intervention.

Today, there are human beings who have to be involved for these tactical decisions. Increasingly, all of those platforms and systems will become automated so that tactical decision making will become something that humans are less involved with. This means humans need to be more involved with big strategic and hard decisions. Should we even offer a product? Should we offer a different line of service? How should we think about our non-line existence? Kaushik explains the importance of critical thinking:

> I think there are very good careers to be had in the near future. It's important to think as you build out your skill set, your children build out their skill set, that they get courses that help them develop an ability to sync multiplicity. To be flexible and agile in their thinking! The future will need people that are more comfortable thinking strategically; who are comfortable with incomplete information; who are comfortable and very fast on their feet; who can think that 2 + 2 can also be 63, or be open to the possibility that it might be.

Kaushik believes that these critical thinking free thinkers are the people who will thrive in the world of Big Data above and beyond the traditional programming and engineering path. The main reason he expounds upon is that we're not in the business of tactical decision making; systems will take care of it.

We're getting in the business of thinking about strategy and thinking about places where logic doesn't work and computers are not good.

—Avinash Kaushik

Analytic Talent and Executive Buy-in

We also sat down with one of the legends in the analytics industry, Marcia Tal, Founder of Tal Solutions, LLC and formerly head of Citi's Decision Management organization. Tal was one of the first business executives to create a centralized analytics organization that cut across all lines of business at a major institution, which she called "decision management"—a term she coined.

Sometimes companies bury analytic teams in silos, which limits their ability to align and influence executive direction and strategy. Not in this case. Tal led more than a "team"; she led the global function filled with top analytic talent and had a direct connection to the top of the house. Tal shared some insightful comments that reinforced the point that there is a plethora of technology and data, but the analytic resources (people) are the keys to the kingdom. Let's hear it in her words:

One of the most interesting opportunities of our times is the dynamic nature of the technological capabilities available for business in almost every sector that you could imagine.

The technology provides access to a vast amount of usable information, but companies haven't yet mastered how to integrate that information and those technology capabilities to create relevant context. The relevancy and context that would come out of that will actually help transform their businesses.

For example, if a business is looking for ways to find new revenue streams, which is a hot topic among may businesses today, they need to find these new revenue streams organically, or inorganically (acquisition), or from a revenue-sharing partnership model.

In order to be able to make the necessary trade-offs for those kinds of decisions, sets of information need to be expertly prepared. At the end of the day, those information sets may be as simple as scenario planning or financial modeling, or based on client segmentation, origination models, and retention models.

Business people must be able to take a forward-looking view of their portfolio, the broader universe, their market potential, and their target market.

It all comes down to the context of the information. Someone has to put that information into simple English business scenarios. And people that can do that are rare!

These exceptionally skilled people understand the business and the input and output of the information that's required to find relevance and context on which solid business decisions can be based. Many leaders are not asking their leadership teams to do this. They don't have the people or organization set up with the role and responsibility of providing that type of information for them.

The bottom line of Tal's observations comes down to people and analytic talent. Tal, like others in this field, truly believes that all applicable companies should have an executive role "chief analytics officer." Marcia explains why that position needs to be at the C-level:

I don't see a chief analytic officer's role as being a backend role, by any means. The chief analytics officer is the person in the center, and therefore their role is to bring new techniques and capabilities to all parts of the businesses so the businesses can identify new insights and new target markets, new segments, new clients, and continuous opportunities for growth. I don't see the chief analytics officer as one

who's experimenting. I see a person that has a huge, huge responsibility to deliver the business's P&L.

Developing Decision Sciences Talent

Mu Sigma, the world's largest decision sciences company, took a much different approach to acquiring talent—they created it. While other companies
struggled to find, recruit, and retain talent, Mu Sigma created a university that
fed their overall business with the talent they needed. The analytical talent
that needed to be "created" by the firm couldn't be "acquired" from outside,
because they don't exist in abundance in the market. Dhiraj Rajaram, CEO of
Mu Sigma, explains:

> We interviewed Ph.D.s in applied math, business majors with many
> years of experience in specific domain areas, technologists with years
> of experience in a variety of technical areas. But somehow, not many
> could internalize the vision that we had for the industry and for Mu
> Sigma. Our beliefs were very different from the state of the industry
> at that time. After a lot of effort, we hand-picked our initial team
> members. These initial members have played a major role in taking
> us from a small start-up to a 2,000 people strong organization that
> lives and breathes decision sciences every day.
>
> Building an analytically strong organization that is focused on
> helping people make better, faster, data-driven decisions, wouldn't
> have been possible without a holistic view of decision sciences. One
> of the key learnings that we had in the initial days of Mu Sigma is
> that analytics had been made into an occult science [knowledge of
> the hidden] in the market and we needed to first break that myth if
> we wanted to build an industry that will make data-driven decision
> making commonplace in any organization.
>
> As long as it is considered an occult science, the adoption of ana-
> lytics for daily decision making in organizations will be limited. If we
> add to that the problem of exponential increases in data, it becomes
> evident to us that our vision to institutionalize analytics will not be
> fulfilled if we don't create a holistic view of analytics, figure out how
> to "create" analytical talent, think about consumption of analytics,
> develop processes that will be scalable and sustainable, and innovate
> along the way as we reach new milestones in our journey to build this
> industry.

They built the Mu Sigma University program to create analytical talent with specific roles to ensure the success of analytic projects.

Analytics education has started and will continue to evolve into a more formalized market in the future. University of Ottawa, North Carolina State University, and DePaul University have started offering formal degree programs in analytics. As companies begin to leverage analytics more and more, they will recognize the need to create and develop talent in this space, providing support to universities to build formal degree programs in analytics. Mature organizations will augment the formal education with their own corporate analytics programs. This will bring in domain knowledge and business context to effectively use analytics in their organizations.

One of the shortcomings of analytics educational programs is that they tend to focus only on analytics techniques, applications, technologies, and data; essentially, the data science aspect of decision sciences. Ideally, more holistic educational programs should recognize the key imperatives and challenges for making decision sciences successful in an organizational context, and will create programs for different roles that come together to enable data-driven decision making.

As we discussed earlier, data-driven decision making is a journey and without the right talent across organizational levels, the benefits of decision sciences cannot be truly realized. We believe decision sciences education is in a nascent stage and needs to evolve to a holistic approach to create the right kind of talent. What is needed is an interdisciplinary approach drawing its foundation from mathematics, business, technology, and behavioral sciences.

Holistic View of Analytics

In the endeavor to become data-driven, organizations need a systematic framework to think about the different types of analytics needed to create insights and help make better decisions.

The framework (shown in Figure 6.3) describes the different kinds of analytics needed:

- **Descriptive analytics.** Answers the question "What happened in the business?" It is looking at data and information to describe the current business situation in a way that trends, patterns, and exceptions become apparent.
- **Inquisitive analytics.** Answers the question "Why is something happening in the business?" It is the study of data to validate/reject business hypotheses.
- **Predictive analytics.** Answers the question "What is likely to happen in the future?" It is data modeling to determine future possibilities.

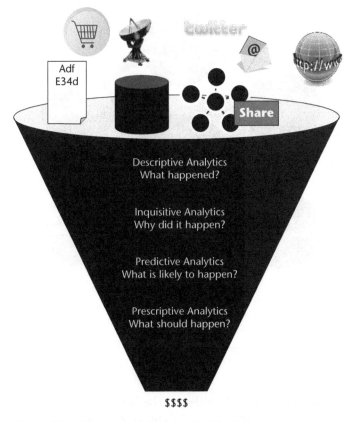

Figure 6.3 Categories of Analytics for Big Data

- **Prescriptive analytics.** Answers a combination of the previous questions to provide answers to the "so what?" and the "now what?" questions, such as "What should I do to retain my key customers?" and "How do I improve my supply chain to enhance service levels while reducing my costs?"

This is not a linear journey; all four kinds of analytics can and should be combined in the right mix. Organizations that focus on only one aspect of analytics will fail to generate the right insights and recommendations.

However, the creation of insights alone is not sufficient. Going forward, companies will compete not so much on the creation of insights, but rather on the consumption of insights. Consumption entails communicating insights, implementing insights, measuring, incentivizing, and developing cognitive repairs.

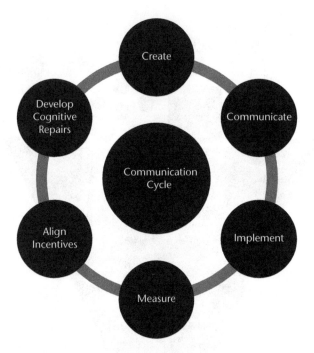

Figure 6.4 Communication Cycle

The communication cycle refers to the planned, ongoing use of a set of interlocking business practices and competencies that collectively deliver superior value from analytics insights. Enabling consumption will need an appreciation of behavioral sciences and how organizations and human beings absorb new and often counter-intuitive insights and process them—or auto-mated processes—to make decisions (see Figure 6.4).

The future of analytics will not just be based on applied math, business, and technology, as it is today. The future will witness the notion of analytics evolving to decision sciences encompassing Math + Business + Technology + Behavioral Sciences.

Creating Talent for Decision Sciences

Creating an analytics culture of data-driven, evidence-based decision making requires new decision science knowledge, skills, and values. Table 6.1 shows the key professional traits required in every member of the team to make decision sciences sustainable.

Table 6.1   Professional Traits Required for Decision Sciences

Necessary Traits	Description
Learning over knowing	Ability to apply first principles and structured approaches to problem solving as opposed to relying excessively on past domain expertise
Agility	Ability to cope with continuous transformation
Scale and convergence	Synergistic ecosystem of talent, capabilities, processes, customers, and partners that can be leveraged across verticals, domains, and geographies
Multidisciplinary talent	Ability to apply business, math, technology, and behavioral sciences
Innovation	Increase breadth and depth of problem solving by constantly researching and deploying emerging techniques, technologies, and applications
Cost effectiveness	Ensure sustainability and institutionalization of problem solving across organizations

At Mu Sigma University, that army of decision science talent emerges from a rigorous program with specific roles:

- **Soldiers.** These are typically analysts and data scientists who work on solving business problems, generating and then communicating findings and insights. Soldiers come from varied backgrounds, including engineering, computer science, economics, math, statistics, business, and other quantitatively oriented fields. They develop skills in analytics techniques, data, technologies, and applications along with a combination of consultative first principles–based thinking for problem definition and hypothesis-based approaches. They also bring together right- and left-brained thinking to balance the rigor of science with the creativity that business requires. Principles of design, usability, and visualization are key to making them successful both in the creation of insights and consumption enablement.
- **Captains.** These are middle managers driving analytical initiatives. They are usually quantitatively oriented professionals with experience in both analytics and functional roles such as marketing, risk, supply chain, and so on. Agile and iterative project management skills required for analytics are essential to adapt to the dynamism of the business problem environment and to manage new processes that cut

across functional boundaries. They also need to develop knowledge management frameworks leveraging insights from across verticals and domains to drive innovation in addition to effectiveness and efficiency. The ability to work with geographically dispersed teams is also a key requirement in a world of "glo-calization," where bringing local perspectives will be essential to success in developing and emerging markets. These captains play a pivotal role in the consumption of analytics since they simultaneously play the role of explaining the science behind the analytics to the business user and translating findings into insights and recommendations. Consequently, an understanding of behavioral sciences and the role of cognitive biases in decision making is key.

- **Generals.** These are senior management folks with a strong vision and passion for data-driven decision making. They come from diverse backgrounds and are organizational leaders with deep business acumen and an appreciation of data-based insights. They develop skills in creating and running cross-functional analytics councils, shared services ecosystems, governance models for analytics organizations, analytics road maps, and so on. Change management and the ability to bridge the gap between creation and consumption of insights is their key focus.

Creating a Culture That Nurtures Decision Sciences Talent

Creating analytical talent is not a one-time effort but a continuous process. This talent needs to be groomed and nurtured in an environment where art and science can exist in harmony.

Mu Sigma has adopted key principles in their recruitment process, training program through Mu Sigma University, appraisal philosophy, and pretty much in everything they do. The principles are from the following thought leaders:

- **Daniel H. Pink, the motivation theory author.** According to Pink, organizations can achieve excellence when their employees are driven by intrinsic motivation and not extrinsic motivation. Organizations need to create a culture that focuses on our innate need for autonomy (freedom over some or all aspects of work), mastery (to learn and create new things), and purpose (focus on the higher purpose that is larger than oneself).

- **Carol S. Dweck, professor of psychology at Stanford and a researcher in fixed versus growth mindsets.** Those with a fixed mind-set believe their talents and abilities cannot be improved through any means. They feel that they are born with a certain amount of talent and typically do not wish to challenge their abilities due to the possibility of failure. Individuals with a fixed mindset frequently guard themselves against situations in which they feel they need to prove their personal worth. Challenges are frequently viewed negatively, instead of as an opportunity for personal growth. People who practice a growth mind-set believe abilities, such as athleticism and mathematical capacity, can be improved through hard work and persistence. When presented with an obstacle, those practicing a growth mind-set tend to rise to the challenge. Often, people of the growth mind-set do not fear failure; instead, they view it as a chance to improve themselves.
- **Maria Montessori, physician, educator, and founder of the Montessori approach to learning.** This approach is characterized by "an emphasis on independence, freedom within limits, and respect for a child's natural psychological development, as well as technological advancements in society."

For example, new hires at the business analyst level start at the same salary. They all go through a rigorous training course; that is, a mini-MBA program in which they learn not just about how the firm does business and services clients, but also review mathematical, communication, and business fundamentals to ensure they have the proper foundation for serving our clients. Then, at the eighteen-month point, these new hires are promoted as a group to senior business analysts, again at the same salary.

During the first three years, managers regularly provide employees with one-on-one feedback, discussing areas for improvement and growth opportunities. It's only after this period that we begin to differentiate (and reward) employees based on their now-proven abilities. Prior to the Montessori model, their managers used promotions as carrots. Now they are challenged to motivate employees in other ways—by giving them interesting projects to work on, public praise for their work, and the right guidance and encouragement.

If you are considering implementing a similar program at your company, here are some lessons learned by the Mu Sigma management:

- **When it comes to new employees, focus on nurturing, not labeling.** Deliberately give all new employees the same title and salary to remove extrinsic measurements of success. You could try this, or find a more subtle way to avoid prematurely labeling an employee's talents.

- **Be sure to give employees room to grow.** Provide them with challenges and let them rise to the occasion. Make it clear that failure is okay as long as they learn something.
- **Emphasize striving for a personal best.** You don't want new hires to compete with each other. Instead, encourage them to continually strive for a personal best—constant improvement of their own skills.

Setting Up the Right Organizational Structure for Institutionalizing Analytics

While there is a lot of focus on analytics from the C-suite today, organizations are looking at it in a siloed manner (see Figure 6.5). The power of analytics can be fully leveraged only if there is collaboration among teams around generation and consumption of insights across the organization.

In typical large organizations, there is fear around collaboration and overreliance on proprietary information.

Overcoming these issues and setting up an organizational structure that takes into account the DNA of the organization, the culture, and overall goals is important. The following are structures that we have seen across many organizations. Each of them has their own pros and cons and the C-suite needs to carefully look into their organizational DNA and select one that is appropriate for them (see Figure 6.6):

1. **Centralized analytics.** A single team that owns the data and services all the analytical needs across all the business functions. While this carries the promise of an integrated data infrastructure and the economies of scale, a centralized model will not be able to provide the agility and flexibility that is required to keep analytics relevant within the business.
2. **Decentralized analytics.** Each business function owns its own data infrastructure and analytics team. While this ensures the agility and flexibility, this model runs the risk of creating different functions within an organization that choose to adopt their respective sets of tools and methodologies. While this approach gets each function off the ground quickly, it runs the risk of creating redundancies or worse, conflicting approaches ultimately resulting in fiefdoms.
3. **Federated model.** This seeks to marry the advantages of both the centralized and the decentralized models. While each function is allowed the flexibility to deploy analytics, a governing council ensures that there is broad alignment on data policies and infrastructure.

Organizations are limited by fear of collaboration and overreliance on proprietary information

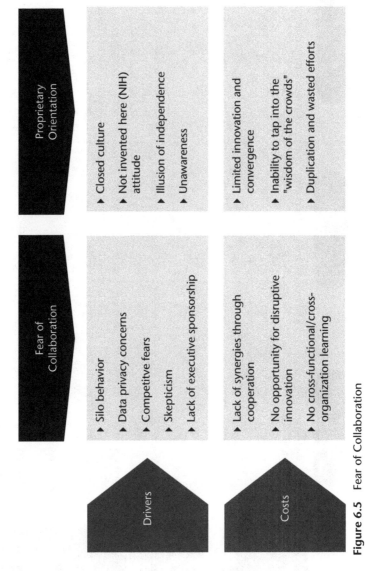

Drivers

Fear of Collaboration
- Silo behavior
- Data privacy concerns
- Competitve fears
- Skepticism
- Lack of executive sponsorship

Proprietary Orientation
- Closed culture
- Not invented here (NIH) attitude
- Illusion of independence
- Unawareness

Costs

Fear of Collaboration
- Lack of synergies through cooperation
- No opportunity for disruptive innovation
- No cross-functional/cross-organization learning

Proprietary Orientation
- Limited innovation and convergence
- Inability to tap into the "wisdom of the crowds"
- Duplication and wasted efforts

Figure 6.5 Fear of Collaboration

147

Different forms of organizational structure will emerge best suited to the analytical needs of the organization

	Centralized	Decentralized	Federated
Description	▸ Central shared services organization serving multiple departments 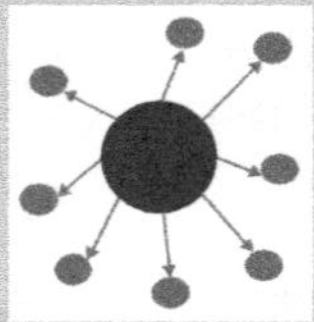	▸ Each department with its own analytics unit 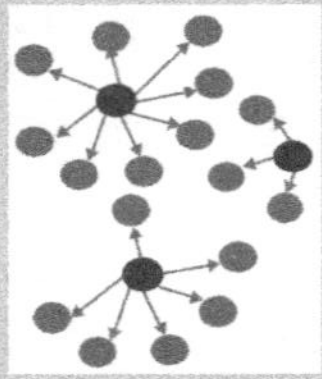	▸ Central coordination with local execution 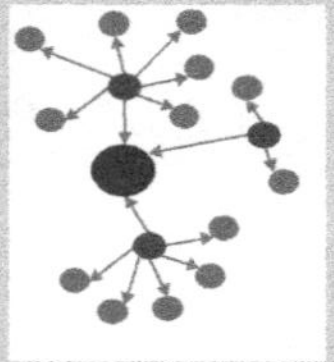
Owner	▸ C-level executive	▸ Business unit/functional heads	▸ C level executive with a team of lieutenants embedded within the business units
Pros	▸ Economies of scale in infrasturcture and process ▸ Ease of promoting a corporate vision of analytics in service of strategic capabilities ▸ Cross functional collaboration	▸ Not aligned with the business units ▸ Risk of spreading too thin in areas that need in depth focus	▸ Retains the agility ▸ Access to the right breadth and depth of skills needed ▸ Autonomy of functional units maintained
Cons	▸ Seen as a cost center ▸ Not aligned with the business units ▸ Slow and Inflexible	▸ Local/silo approach ▸ Short term focus ▸ Lack of control and alignment to corporate vision	▸ Coordination and planning are easier said than done

Figure 6.6 Analytic Team Models

Needless to say, this model is extremely hard to execute and requires commitment from the leadership.

Data-driven decision making is a journey, and without the right talent across organizational levels, the benefits of decision sciences cannot be truly realized. What is needed is an interdisciplinary approach, drawing its foundation from mathematics, business, technology, and behavioral sciences and a culture that nurtures the talent and drives innovation.

In today's business world, every company is seeking to leverage analytics for their business. Yet, as it often happens in an evolving discipline, companies that are investing in analytics often find that the businesses do not consume the outputs for a variety of reasons. And as companies realize that one of the many factors that separate failure from success is their ability to effectively use analytics to make better decisions, it becomes necessary for the key stakeholders to ensure the right set of investments are made on the process, technology, and people dimensions to bridge the gap between the creation and consumption of analytics.

The sooner businesses can get this done, the better their chances are of leveraging the potential competitive advantage offered by analytics.

CHAPTER 7

Data Privacy and Ethics

The current Big Data surge has predominantly been driven by a never-ending deluge of online clicks, queries, and paths: the artifacts of online activity. Debates have been going on for years and will continue as we work out the wrinkles between "rights"—the individual's rights to determine what personal information he or she is willing to "barter" in exchange for free services versus the service provider's rights to determine how to continue to provide free services. It's a basic matter of quid pro quo—a mutual agreement of exchange of value. As with any relationship, there will always be squabbles around everyone's interpretation of said agreements.

In a personal one-on-one relationship, two parties mutually work out the details of an exchange and agreement. In the case of online (digital product/service) agreements, the individual has only one immediate binary choice: accept the terms as stated or forego the service. There's generally no negotiation or setting conditional exchanges. Then again, this is not much different than product agreements in the past.

The fact of the matter is most people don't comprehend the computational power and possibilities that Big Data brings. Some think it would be impossible for someone to glean deep insight into their private lives. Big Data makes it harder to keep secrets. Jeff Jonas, IBM Chief Scientist, posted in his blog "Using Transparency as a Mask":

> Unlike two decades ago, humans are now creating huge volumes of extraordinarily useful data as they self-annotate their relationships and yours, their photographs and yours, their thoughts and their thoughts about you ... and more. With more data comes better understanding and prediction. The convergence of data might reveal your "discreet" rendezvous or the fact that you are no longer on speaking terms with your best friend. Pity ... you thought that all of this information was secret.

Table 7.1   Privacy Landscape

Businesses	■ Increased need to leverage personally identifiable and sensitive information for competitive advantage
	■ Significant investment in data sources and data analytics
Criminals	■ Dramatic surge in identity theft
	■ Sophisticated technology to exploit data security vulnerabilities
Consumers	■ Increased awareness and concern about collection, use, and disclosure of their personal information
Legislators	■ Responding to consumer concern by restricting access to and use of personal information
	■ Significant impact and restriction for business

Source: Adapted from Andrew Reiskind.

The Privacy Landscape

There are four main constituents involved in the privacy landscape. Table 7.1 shows how they are impacted.

The Great Data Grab Isn't New

While there are critical differences between digital product agreements and their "analog" counterparts, there are historical similarities worth considering briefly. While data volumes are clearly greater today, the great data grab has been going on for decades. One primary means of past data exchange was via the warranty card that came with products. Under the guise of registering a product to ensure warranty rights, companies gathered personal information about individuals. These cards were not managed by the companies themselves but were outsourced to processing centers, which then had access to data across products. They gladly bundled and sold this data to other companies.

What began as list brokering evolved into the field of database marketing, which added analytics and attempted to address the differences between channels to better "target" exchanges with consumers. Over time, the marketplace of physical products was dwarfed by "services as products," such as banking, telecommunications, and the like. These services industries relied even more on such data to not only offer the right products to consumers but to change their products to better meet consumer need.

For years, big companies paid millions to brokers to provide segmented lists (created using data mining scoring algorithms, assessing specific behavioral tendencies). The process was long and tedious: the turn cycle for new data was often six months or more.

Then in the mid-1990s, data warehousing made it feasible for such companies to "roll their own." MCI, which managed nearly 300 million individuals in their Friends & Family database, was able to bring their data in-house, on their own data warehouse for the same cost as their annual list broker (in this case, Epsilon) outsourcing fees—and they were able to update the data monthly rather than every six months. This meant that data going into the call centers was far more accurate (not to mention that in the process of the transition, it was discovered that one of the twenty algorithmic scores being used by the outsourcing vendor had a flaw in it and had been providing inaccurate results).

In the mid-1990s the sources of data that MCI leveraged went well beyond the lone warranty card. While they still used data from the list brokers they also used: updates from the U.S. Postal Service, "partner" relationships with other companies that offered affinity exchanges (airlines offering miles for minutes), and credit data (although the latter was dropped when new regulations were put in place that made it difficult to "use" the data). Unfortunately, neither their databases nor their operations were designed to truly leverage the data they could have gotten directly from their own consumers. They spent inordinate time and money using algorithms to "predict" behaviors rather than simply allowing their own customers to share their preferences.

Preferences, Personalization, and Relationships

As database marketing gave way to Customer Relationship Management (CRM) and one-to-one marketing, the focus shifted from segmentation to personalizing relationships: The more you knew about a consumer, the better you could meet their needs.

There are many reasons why we as consumers are perfectly willing to provide personal data (including specifying preferences) in doing business: Used responsibly, it can enhance our exchange. Indeed, we are often frustrated by dealing with companies that don't "know" us as individuals, that don't combine our information across products, across organizational boundaries, and across channels, and that don't remember anything about the last interaction we had with them. When attempting to resolve issues, we tire quickly of having to repeat ourselves and re-create yet again the details of our relationship with the company. This is the flipside of the coin—companies not collecting "enough" information about us.

If we are doing business with a company, there is a relationship that we've inherently agreed to. But we also expect that companies will respect and not abuse the information we share with them. And we're particularly leery of companies asking us for personal information before we've decided that we want to do business with them at all (flash back to bad online site designs asking for "registration" before you've even seen what they're all about). That's like asking for a marriage license before the first date.

And yet, like with a marriage relationship we often feel like we've woken up next to a stranger—that the relationship we thought we had seems foreign to what it is we're now experiencing. As with relationships, this alienation is often due to three key factors:

1. Nonsustained or nondifferentiating memory (not remembering what's important to an individual)
2. Lagging empathy (missing consideration for needs)
3. Inability to "listen" and process what's been heard (insufficient mechanisms for individuals to engage in conversations and see corresponding change/results)

These concerns go way beyond the growing industry focus on privacy. We raise them here just as a matter of setting a larger scope for the realm in which privacy policies fit and to reiterate that they're in support of something larger and more meaningful: a relationship. Privacy is the fallback for the "low bar to entry" in relationships—it's more about the "have to do" rather than the "need to do."

Rights and Responsibility

A consumer privacy bill of rights is a critical public policy proposal. I have long advocated for consumer privacy protections and will continue to push for legislation because I believe consumer privacy is a right, not a luxury. Above all else, it is absolutely crucial that, as we move forward in an evolving online and mobile world, consumer choice is protected and preserved. I will work to do just that.

—Senator John D. (Jay) Rockefeller

The expression "data is the new oil" certainly couldn't be any more fitting when Senator Jay Rockefeller gets involved in the Big Data world. As a great-grandson of oil tycoon John D. Rockefeller, Senator Rockefeller, at this writing, serves as the chairman of the Committee on Commerce, Science, and Transportation. Senator Rockefeller and other senators, such as John Kerry, have been quite aggressive in their efforts to protect consumers from companies abusing their access to private data.

Senator Rockefeller helped pioneer one of the key bills approved by the White House, which is the "Do Not Track Bill." This bill gives the FTC the power to create a "Do Not Track" database so people could opt out of online tracking. According to *InformationWeek*, the "Do Not Track" came about from a Mozilla Firefox add-on prototype, which added headers to outgoing HTTP requests: "XBehavioral-Ad-Opt-Out" and "X-Do-Not-Track." Interestingly enough, this only applies to browsers; mobile devices can still be tracked.[1]

So what can companies do with all the personal data they collect? And how do we know that they're doing what they say they will? When exactly are our rights violated? Why should it matter to us?

Oddly, there was national policy put in place way before most of us had even heard of the Internet. In 1986, an Electronic Communication Privacy Act (ECPA) set boundaries for access to personal information by law enforcement. In 2000, the Children's Online Protection Privacy Act went into effect. It protects the online activity of all children under the age of thirteen from being tracked at all and no personal information to be gathered without parental consent. While privacy rights are specifically protected for health information (HIPAA: Health Insurance Portability and Accountability Act of 1996) and financial services (Gramm–Leach–Bliley Act (GLB), also known as the Financial Services Modernization Act of 1999), there really are no specific laws protecting online privacy, although a number of bills continue to attempt to make their way through legislation, such as H.R. 1528: Consumer Privacy Protection Act of 2011.

While the Federal Trade Commission (FTC) has a set of online privacy guidelines that it enforces, online privacy is largely a matter of exchange between consumers and those they do business with—they're effectively self-regulated, although there is some state regulation such as the California Office of Privacy Protection's requirement for an agency, person, or business that conducts business in California and owns or licenses computerized "personal information" to disclose any breach of security.

The truth is that most companies develop their own privacy policies as a matter of establishing a modicum of "trust" with consumers. There are several variations of seven principles outlined in the "EU-US Safe Harbor

Principles," which most companies have engrained into their self-regulation for data privacy:

Seven Global Privacy Principles

1. **Notice (Transparency):** Inform individuals about the purposes for which information is collected
2. **Choice:** Offer individuals the opportunity to choose (or opt out) whether and how personal information they provide is used or disclosed
3. **Consent:** Only disclose personal data information to third parties consistent with the principles of notice and choice
4. **Security:** Take responsible measures to protect personal information from loss, misuse, and unauthorized access, disclosure, alteration, and destruction
5. **Data Integrity:** Assure the reliability of personal information for its intended use and reasonable precautions and ensure information is accurate, complete, and current
6. **Access:** Provide individuals with access to personal information data about them
7. **Accountability:** A firm must be accountable for following the principles and must include mechanisms for assuring compliance[2]

Self-governance may soon change. In February 2012, the White House announced an initiative to protect privacy under the "Consumer Privacy Bill of Rights." To be initiated by the Commerce Department, and developed in conjunction with Internet companies and consumer advocate groups, it will be enforced by the FTC:

> American Internet users should have the right to control personal information about themselves. Based on globally accepted privacy principles originally developed in the United States, the Consumer Privacy Bill of Rights is a comprehensive statement of the rights consumers should expect and the obligations to which companies handling personal data should commit. These rights include the right to control how personal data is used, the right to avoid having information collected in one context and then used for an unrelated purpose, the right to have information held securely, and the right to know who is accountable for the use or misuse of an individual's personal data.[3]

That said, this is still a voluntary act, not legislation. According to *CNN Money*, "The Administration supports Federal legislation that adopts the principles of the Consumer Privacy Bill of Rights. Even without legislation, the Administration is convening multistakeholder processes that use these rights as a template for codes of conduct that are enforceable by the Federal Trade Commission."[4]

Other than HIPAA and GLB, the only real legislative action that can be taken (in 2012) is where the FTC steps in to require a company to honor its stated privacy policy.

Attention to privacy policies took a spike in March 2012 when Google announced plans to merge their sixty different privacy policies (separate ones for various services) into one. What appeared to raise the most concern was not so much the merging of the policies but the implied merging of the data associated with the different services. This rang vaguely familiar to a point in history over a decade earlier when DoubleClick (which had *a lot* of clickstream data) bought Abacus Direct (a company that knew a lot about our offline buying habits). The potential for merging such data got the attention of watchdog groups such as the Electronic Privacy Information Center, which then got the FTC involved ending in a settlement.

Speaking of settlements, Google ended up in another snafu with DoubleClick, which it acquired in 2008, by creating a technological loophole that enabled the DoubleClick advertising network to shadow unwitting Apple Safari users. This resulted in the largest FTC privacy penalty ever. According to an FTC posting on August 9, 2012:

> Google Inc. has agreed to pay a record $22.5 million civil penalty to settle Federal Trade Commission charges that it misrepresented to users of Apple Inc.'s Safari Internet browser that it would not place tracking "cookies" or serve targeted ads to those users, violating an earlier privacy settlement between the company and the FTC.
>
> The settlement is part of the FTC's ongoing efforts to make sure companies live up to the privacy promises they make to consumers, and is the largest penalty the agency has ever obtained for a violation of a Commission order. In addition to the civil penalty, the order also requires Google to disable all the tracking cookies it had said it would not place on consumers' computers.[5]

It's incidents like this that prompted a change in career focus for attorney Andrew Reiskind, Managing Counsel, Privacy and Data Protection for MasterCard. Reiskind shares his perspectives on the topic of privacy by first clarifying what it means:

> Privacy is about how you use personal data. It's the conscious choice about how that information is used. We usually bucket it into the collection of data, the use of that data, and the disclosure of that data— to whom are you giving that data?

Personal information (PI) is a term that Reiskind notes has changed meaning over time:

Historically, we've always thought of it as a full name—a first name and a last name—a postal address and a phone number. Over time it's now included an e-mail address, a facsimile number, and a government-issued identification number (e.g., SSN). It's moved along that spectrum to things like static IP addresses, which years ago nobody would have ever considered to be personal information. Cookie IDs in many instances are now considered personal information, as well as financial account numbers. For example, although a financial account number by itself, couldn't identify an individual, it is still unique to an individual, and because it is unique to an individual, that's what makes it personally identifiable. It's not about actually identifying somebody, but it's about data being unique to the individual, that is "identifiable."

Individual states have gotten involved in determining what constitutes personally identifiable information. It is against California state law for retailers to ask patrons for their ZIP codes for marketing purposes, and Massachusetts enacted similar legislation in 2011.

In addition to personal information there's concern for the use and collection of "sensitive information," which Reiskind expounds upon:

It's generally information that could cause harm or embarrassment to an individual. We think of things like healthcare information as something being potentially embarrassing to an individual. Sexual orientation is another example of something that we consider sensitive. What is sensitive is contextual. For example, with respect to financial information in the United States, we consider pretty private what you make as income. That's not necessarily true in other geographies.

In another example, in Europe, trade union membership is considered sensitive data. However, here in the United States, we don't really think of it as such. It comes of class associations with trade union membership and therefore it is a sensitive data point.

Sensitive data is collected with PI. In certain countries and markets, additional restrictions apply to collection, use, or disclosure of sensitive data. Note that many companies have sensitive data policies, but that such policies may be focused on data that is sensitive to the company itself, and it may or may not include reference to personally sensitive data. From the perspective of data management policies, differentiating and managing such data appropriately is a matter of *data classification*.

Let's explore the differences between personally identifiable information, sensitive information, and other information as described in Table 7.2.

Playing in a Global Sandbox

Indeed, it would appear that the United Kingdom and the EU have a more comprehensive legislative approach to matters of data privacy than the United States. In 1998, the United Kingdom established the Data Protection Act, which very specifically addresses issues of personal and sensitive data and which is overseen and enforced by a Data Protection Commissioner. This was the United Kingdom's response to the EU's 1995 Data Protection Directive.

As suggested by Andrew Reiskind in the previous section, companies that operate globally have a lot of unexpected implications to consider, including and especially cultural ones. We might not consider how factors of daily human exchange play into such differences, such as lower-income environments in which entire families share a cell phone (not unlike the way people shared a single household landline). Their sense of privacy and where they draw boundaries is entirely different to situations where each family member has one or more personal mobile device.

These are contextual factors—factors that affect perceptions of privacy. Whether global or local our contexts are constantly changing. Individuals

Table 7.2 Types of Protected Information

Personally Identifiable Information (PII): any information that directly or indirectly identifies a person	Sensitive Information: any information whose unauthorized disclosure could be embarrassing or detrimental to the individual	Other Information: any other nonidentifiable information about an individual when combined with PII
Name	Race/ethnicity	Preferences
Postal address	Political opinions	Cookie ID
Email address	Religious/philosophical beliefs	Static IP address
Telephone/mobile number	Trade union membership	
Social Security Number	Health/medical information	
Driver's license number	Marital status/sexual life	
Bank/financial account	Age	
Credit or debit card number	Gender	
ZIP Code	Criminal record	

inherently adopt different postures of trust and willingness to share depending on those contexts. What we share in one context we might clearly object to being shared in another. The more recent issues with Google's collapsing of privacy policies are heavily influenced by concerns over contextual relevance: What's relevant in one context is not relevant in another.

Academics from Dublin, Ireland, to Pittsburgh, Pennsylvania (note the implied global breadth), have shown the significance of context by referencing the concept of contextual integrity (CI). The CI concept was developed as an alternate benchmark for evaluating privacy breaches.

Contexts model societal structure, reflecting the core concept that society has distinctive settings. For example, society distinguishes between the social contexts of a hospital and a university. CI allows individuals to describe their privacy expectations by associating norms of behavior with contexts. The notion of a context and its norms mirror societal structure. In contrast to other privacy theories, CI associates the context with the subject's attribute being passed. Whether or not the data in question is confidential is often not the issue—information may only be deemed sensitive with respect to certain contexts.

Authors Caroline Sheedy and Ponnurangam Kumaragur note that such contexts include not only geolocation relative to specific operating contexts (a hospital versus a university) but also the relevance of such information to specific individuals and their roles within those contexts. These variables change relative to the collection versus the dissemination of such information. The most classic example of a role within a specific context and the collection and dissemination of information is that of information shared with a clergyman in the context of a "confession." This can just as easily be seen in the context of a university student that is receiving financial aid. There are many with a "need to know" to operationalize the disbursement of such financial aid, but there is also a limit to the use of such information within that context.[6] The authors note that there have been cultural indexes developed to help show key differences in cultural perceptions of privacy.

G. J. Hofstede developed a number of cultural indices that measure the differences between societies. Of particular relevance is the Individualism Index (IDV), which measures how collectivist or individualist a society is. As India has a low IDV score, it is considered a collectivist society. Collectivist societies consider harmony with one's social environment a key virtue. Group interests prevail over those of the individual. In contrast to this, the United States is the highest ranking individualist society in Hofstede's study.

The applicability of this index to privacy was further validated in a 2010 study at Carnegie Mellon University, where even controlling for age and gender differences, the distinctions between cultures (American, Chinese, and Indian) were significant:

U.S. users tend to be the most privacy concerned among all, followed by Chinese users. Indian users were the least privacy concerned. . . . Phone number, residence street address, e-mail address, photo, and employer were considered as privacy sensitive by more than half of both the U.S. and Chinese respondents. However, only phone number was considered privacy sensitive by more than half of the Indian respondents.[7]

Then there are the hard differentiators between countries themselves on the topic. Whereas in the United States, the topic is generally referred to as "Privacy Policy," in Europe they focus on "Data Protection." Google's 2012 policy rollup was not well-received in the United Kingdom, where their Deputy Information Commissioner insisted that it was "too vague." In his statement, he wrote, "The requirement under the UK Data Protection Act is for a company to tell people what it actually intends to do with their data, not just what it might do at some unspecified point in future. . . . Being vague does not help in giving users effective control about how their information is shared. It's their information at the end of the day." Whereas in the United States we're given the right to trade or sell our privacy in exchange for services (a contract right), in the European Union, data protection is viewed as an inalienable right that cannot be removed from a citizen, regardless of which country an agreement is transacted.

Andrew Reiskind adds this insight:

For multinational companies that need to transfer data to the U.S., there are a couple of mechanisms that allow companies to transfer personal information from Europe to the U.S. One of those is Safe Harbor, by which companies self-certify compliance, with certain principals. There are other mechanisms, such as "model contacts." These mechanisms are all intended to protect European personal data no matter where in the world the data is located.

Conscientious and Conscious Responsibility

Contrary to what the newsworthy incidents of privacy failures might suggest, most companies go through considerable effort to be conscientious about their approach to issues of privacy and attempt to avoid violation of individual rights. The issues are actually more aligned to that of consciousness—being aware of the potential consequences and taking steps to mitigate them ... in advance, when possible.

The reality is, as much as modern business attempts to do so, we can't really control all that much. But we can influence results. As noted previously, the best way to manage issues of sensitivity is to simply allow individuals to control what "works for them" and to provide adequate (and accessible) feedback loops that are "active"—where real dialog is exchanged, where feedback is a critical, influencing factor for operational change, and where there is transparency in changes made.

Even in the United Kingdom, their Data Protection Acts may specify such things such as "What is mean by sensitive personal data?" but then add a caveat at the end that says, "The Data Protection Acts require additional conditions to be met for the processing of such data to be legitimate. Usually this will be the consent of the person about whom the data relates."

For those companies that continue to take a parental posture in relationships—"We know what's best for you"—their failures will be heard and debated in the open courts of social exchange. Damage control will be difficult.

Privacy May Be the Wrong Focus

Where it relates to businesses, I think it is so easy to violate privacy that perhaps a better framing for the conversation is one of ethics. Data privacy is the thing you do to keep from getting sued, data ethics is the thing you do to make your relationship with your customers positive.

—James Stogdill, O'Reilly Radar

There are many examples of where the focus isn't just about privacy; it's about what James Stogdill refers to as ethics and a positive customer relationship. For example, there probably isn't a customer in the world that would be okay with an iPhone app that secretly downloaded your entire address book without your consent. That would classify as an intrusive tactic that would certainly irritate even the most liberal social butterflies.

In February 2012, Arun Thampi, a developer in Singapore, was exercising his powers of creativity, preparing to participate in a social "hackathon." He thought he'd work on an iPhone app that leveraged Path, an app for journaling and sharing the paths of one's life. (It sounds vaguely like Twitter's original model: "What are you doing?") Then he noticed requests between the phone and Path's servers, which included a "post" of the entire contents of his phone's address book to Path's server. Ironically, Path's byline is "The simple and private way to share life with family."

He blogged about the "creepiness" factor and the courts of social exchange were now in session.

The comments flew back and forth—most of them exchanges of arm-chair lawyerism, with little accuracy or relevance. The most relevant and actionable violation was against Apple's guidelines for apps to be sold in the iStore. Within hours, the CEO of Path, Dave Morin, stepped in to comment and eventually posted a formal statement on their web site. His statement included details about the actions taken ("We've deleted the entire collection of user uploaded contact information from our servers") and their ongoing commitment to transparency. More important, they fixed their software to give control of such data to the individual: "In Path 2.0.6, released to the App Store today, you are prompted to opt in or out of sharing your phone's contacts with our servers in order to find your friends and family on Path."

The courts of social exchange are expedient (unlike their real world counterparts). This all occurred within the span of 24 hours.

In our interview with Andrew Reiskind, he was very specific to point out that as a privacy attorney he assesses the type of data being collected, how it is going to be used, and how it will be disclosed and shared—it's really a matter of reasonable and responsible use of data. There are some very specific contexts in which we want our personal data to be used. Clearly, we need for a call center representative to look at our account to help us with a problem, but Reiskind shared some other interesting scenarios:

> So as you can imagine with health care information, you want the doctor to be able to use the information to treat you. You want the doctor in an emergency situation to be able to call the hospital and say, "Hello, Andrew is on the way the ER. Here and the things you need to know about him." So there are circumstances and exceptions for which companies would not need to notify or obtain the consent of the consumer about what is being done with their information.
>
> The same is true with sharing information with family members. In a situation where Andrew is unconscious, you would want my spouse to know, "Andrew is unconscious, here's his status …" So there are exceptions to the requirements to provide notice and obtain consent.
>
> The same is true for the financial privacy laws. Again, financial institutions with which consumers have relations (generally your banks), have to tell you what they're going to do with the data and have to abide by that. There are certain, specific exemptions for their use of the data where they don't have to tell you what they're doing

with the data. For example, in order to process a check you used to pay for some goods from a merchant, the merchant's bank needs to use your financial information to process the check you wrote. Again there are exceptions to the requirements of notice and consent to get the financial system to work.

In many other instances there is a need to use information, not for the exact purpose for which it was given, but to use it for ancillary purposes. For example, in the health care industry and the pharmaceutical industry there's a need to understand the adverse reactions to drugs. The pharmaceutical companies need to know someone had a reaction to penicillin because of the specific formulation of penicillin.

In that case, query how do you do that without impacting the privacy of an individual? As a result of those concerns and those desires, there's been a lot of discussion and a lot of work done to say, "Well many of the requirements of applicable privacy laws don't apply to 'anonymized' data."

Can Data Be Anonymized?

The issue at hand is, can data gathered for a specific purpose then be used for other purposes (referred to as, "secondary use") by somehow being stripped of the classification of *personally identifiable information* (PII) and allowing the individuals associated with that data to remain anonymous? Can this non-PII data be generalized for identifying collective patterns when there is no need to get back to an individual?

The simple answer is yes! The challenge is the more you *anonymize* the data, the less utility the data has. There are many that believe that removing identifying information also, inevitably, removes contextual information that has potential value to someone analyzing the data. On the flipside, others point out that it doesn't take much to reconstitute an identity. So what's the point of going through the effort to try to anonymize data to begin with? The same research paper noted that attempting to go through the data to "flag" parts that might be considered PII "would come at the cost of financing actual research ... simply not practical."[8]

It would seem that it comes to a matter of choice: allowing individuals to opt into specific scenarios and applied uses of our data (although the prevalent model in force today is an "opt out" model). Might we not want to contribute to research that requires real data about real people? What if that research saves lives? Or might we all collapse under the weight of granting permission to every permutation of the use of our data and throw our arms up in frustration with it all? Could our desire to want to be informed of all secondary use of our data turn out to be a matter of "Be careful what you ask for"?

Balancing for Counterintelligence

Of course, all paths come with a few unexpected twists, turns, and bumps along the way. On March 22, 2012, the Attorney General signed new guidelines for the "access, use, retention and dissemination" of datasets by the National Counterterrorism Center. These replace guidelines established in 2008. One of the main changes was the extension of data retention from 180 days to five years, purportedly to have a better span of time across which to mine for "patterns that could indicate a threat."

Currently, if a terrorist association is made to a U.S. citizen (e.g., listed as a contact for visa application), to see if that citizen has been listed as a contact for other foreign travelers, requires a request to the State Department to check their databases. Under the new guidelines, the patterns could be detected automatically.

In the open dialog that ensued from this announcement, there was mixed receipt of the information: many self-proclaimed Democrats/Liberals insisting that this administration has done more to banish their privacy rights than any previous one, some suggesting that having privacy rights trampled is the "new normal," and others suggesting that the information in question is already public.

It seems that there will always be a need to balance the reasonable against the unreasonable uses of personal data. The boundaries for such will continue to be tested by new circumstances and scenarios.

Now What?

In the realm of Big Data, companies need to take the time to evaluate and seriously challenge their assumptions about data "ownership," perhaps going so far as to include data attributes to explicitly differentiate where the real authority lies in determining the use of data (versus simply managing it in a security layer, which isn't explicit at all) and the associated permissions that have or have not been granted by those owners.

Recommendations have also been made by academics and professionals to align these management activities to a common middleware layer. For example, Sharad Mehrotra and Bijit Hore, of the Department of Computer Science, University of California–Irvine, explain that "A middleware layer will act as a broker for an individual. It will ensure that the required degree of privacy and confidentiality across a wide cross-section of web applications is implemented and at the same time allow the users to access many of the value added functionalities offered by the service providers."[9] This certainly seems like a viable option to consider for managing the primary use but also the secondary use of data.

In addressing an audience at the 2011 O'Reilly Strata Data Conference, the chief technology officer from Thomson Reuters, James Powell, labeled one major privacy challenge as "ambiguity," or the casual reliance on managing things implicitly. He challenged that there is a need to be more explicit:

> A lot of the problems that are going to happen around privacy and the concerns that are being raised are the leverage of implicit contracts, which are made with the big data miners. As you start to design products that leverage [personal] information ... you need to be careful and make sure that you're explicit about how you're going to use that information.

But he also challenged the upper left quadrant of Figure 7.1 by adding a compelling perspective:

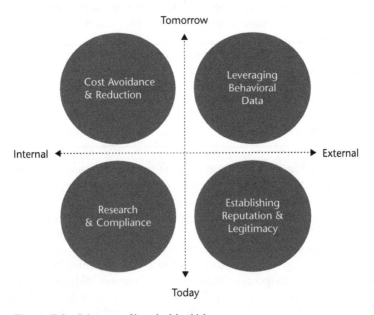

Figure 7.1   Privacy as Shareholder Value
Source: Thomson Reuters.

Rather than look at it as a compliance problem or a cost avoidance problem, you can actually look at it as an opportunity ... an opportunity to do the right thing and build a strong relationship with your customer.

There likely never will be a specific approach or a foolproof strategy for privacy policies and attempting to honor the bonds of trust in a relationship—it will simply keep emerging to adapt to the changing contexts. Being willing to take a position, stand by it, and adapt it as contexts persuade will be most relevant. Committing to relationships and championing a "do no harm" mind-set is key. Recognizing that "do no harm" is never fully achievable requires us to circle back to the need to be positioned to listen and respond appropriately.

Notes

1. Mathew J. Schwartz, "Do Not Track: 7 Key Facts," *InformationWeek*, February 24, 2012, www.informationweek.com/security/privacy/do-not-track-7-key-facts/232601425.
2. Adapted from both International Safe Harbor Privacy Principles and Andrew Reiskind's interview for this book.
3. Barack Obama, "Whitehouse Consumer Data Privacy in a Networked World: A Framework for Protecting Privacy and Promoting innovation in the Global Digital Economy," February 2012.
4. "Consumer Privacy Bill of Rights," *CNNMoneyTech*, February 23, 2012, money.cnn.com/2012/02/22/technology/bill_of_rights_privacy/index.htm.
5. Federal Trade Commission, "Google Will Pay $22.5 Million to Settle FTC Charges It Misrepresented Privacy Assurances to Users of Apple's Safari Internet Browser," FTC Press Release: 08/09/2012, www.ftc.gov/opa/2012/08/google.shtm.
6. Caroline Sheedy and Ponnurangam Kumaraguru. "A Contextual Method for Evaluating Privacy Preferences," in *IFIP International Federation for Information Processing*, vol. 261, Policies and Research in Identity Management (Berlin: Springer, 2008), 139–146.
7. Yang Wang, Gregory Norcie, and Lorrie Faith Cranor, "Who Is Concerned about What? A Study of American, Chinese and Indian Users' Privacy Concerns on Social Network Sites," Short Paper, School of Computer Science, Carnegie Mellon University, 2011, www.cs.cmu.edu/~yangwan1/papers/TRUST2011-%C2%AD-AuthorCopy.pdf.
8. Ibid.
9. Sharad Mehrotra and Bijit Hore, "A Middleware Approach for Managing Privacy of Outsourced Personal Data," Department of Computer Science, University of California–Irvine, 2009, www.utdallas.edu/~jxr061100/papers/nsf2009das_submission_12.pdf.

CONCLUSION

The availability of Big Data, low-cost commodity hardware, and new information management and analytic software have produced a unique moment in the history of data analysis. The convergence of these trends means that we have the capabilities required to analyze astonishing data sets quickly and cost-effectively for the first time in history. These capabilities are neither theoretical nor trivial. They represent a genuine leap forward and a clear opportunity to realize enormous gains in terms of efficiency, productivity, revenue, and profitability.

The Age of Big Data is here, and these are truly revolutionary times if both business and technology professionals continue to work together and deliver on the promise.

Thank you for taking the time to read our book and we hope you enjoyed reading it as much as we did writing it. We'd like to conclude with a transcript from one of the most charismatic speakers on the Big Data circuit, Google's Avinash Kaushik, from his presentation at Strata 2012, "A Big Data Imperative: Driving Big Action":

> I actually don't really care about the promise of data unless they can deliver on that promise that comes with the data.
>
> I'm going to try and bring things back to a practical level and open my talk with this quote, "Information is powerful," said a Kenyan farmer, "it's what we use it for that will define us." I love, I *love* this quote. If you look at all the hype that's connects to big data it solves for the first problem, if you listen to all the vendors, 99 percent of all the speakers, myself included, you'll see there's a lot of emphasis on this first part and little emphasis on the second part. What I do at Google and at other companies is play with one of the largest sources of data in the world, with its websites and entities that more than a billion hits a day and tens of millions and millions of these things. When you play with all that stuff, one of the key things you have to figure out is, how do you make all these pedabytes, terabytes, and zetabytes of data actionable to the person who is sitting on the ground and a lot more useful. I actually don't really care about the promise of data unless they can deliver on that promise that comes with the data.
>
> One of the things that I have figured out is that the model we've used to big data internalized companies has been broken for a very long time. The typical model in the company is that there is a lot of

data, and we "Hadoopify it" and have a lot of sexy fun with it. There are a lot of people who need that data, and some really arrogant ones who believe they don't need to touch data and they will just rely on the "data gods" who work for them.

What we do is we hire these "gods" and "princelings" to take this data converted reports and hopefully pray that they will take action at the other end. The problem with this model is it doesn't actually scale because as the users multiply, we run around like bunnies trying to find people that don't exist, whose job then it is to produce ever-more data and start hitting people with it every single day. They're trying to produce action. It's what ironically what happens is the company becomes more inefficient, not less. A very, very sad, pathetic story.

The things that I like more is the idea of creating a data democracy where you still have all this data and you've figured out how to make love to it. There are all these people, and rather than creating this intermediate layer between them, kind of dump them over there and say you, janitor, you will figure out how to use data every day to do your job better. And you, the marketer, God forbid, will have to figure out how to use data better, and then they're making love to the data directly so that they can make decisions to improve their lives every day. There will still be the arrogant people who refuse to touch data because their faith still sustains them. For them, we will create these princes who will play with it. And the big difference in the scenarios is because you've empowered every person to take power of the data. Very, very large decisions will be made based on the output from the data gods and princelings and all the other actual useful decisions will be made by people closer to the data. And this scales . . . the great thing is this scales, they're a part of every person's job. Having these people in the blue run around like bunnies trying to produce something.

I found that this drives a lot of innovation. Of course, there is always a fly in the ointment. In this case, the problem is that the world in which we live in doesn't look like this, which was very manageable a few years ago when I played with terabyte data houses. But, it actually looks more like this. We still have these people here and now they are scared and cleaning their hands. What is this? Big, freakin' data!

I have found a great solace in trying to figure out how to get rid of this fly in the ointment by one of the greatest philosophers when it comes to data analytics, Donald Rumsfeld. I'm not a big fan of this man but he said one of the greatest things that has really powered my thinking in this space. What he said is, "We screwed up, because in life there are the known knowns." Things we know that we know and the known unknowns—things we know we don't know. We really got hosed because there are things that we don't know that we don't even know. I just love the idea that the entire data world can be boiled down into these three problems. Love, love, that quote and I thank God for creating Donald Rumsfeld for giving me this quote.

When I think about massive people running with their heads cut off in front of data, I frame things into three buckets. My job is to try to figure out how to solve these problems for people so that the world is a better place having used data to make decisions.

When I think about these three things in our daily life, they fall into these three outcomes for me. This is most of our life – we know and we just puke it like hell on things we call dashboards. The known unknowns more fall into the category of analysis throwing . . . the things that I love is this last part. If you could figure this thing out, we could have saved Afghanistan from big problems.

When it comes to data on the Web, the things that I deal with billions and billions of rows of data, what I want to figure out is how to do this better because when I do this better, I can create that. These two things are very closely tied together. You don't do the former, you don't get the latter. The question to me is what is my big data solving for? What is your big data solving for? I've come up with two examples to show you how we try and solve this problem. One is a very super-tactical solution and the other one is big, more strategic–complex. But in both cases, I'm trying to figure out if I have billions of rows of data available to me, how do I actually find the known unknowns? That is a very sexy, complex problem to solve.

The first one is astonishingly simple. It's brilliant. The problem we have is there are massive amounts of data, even for tiny websites I have. In this case, what I want to figure out is a very simple question—the content produces how much money for me? That's available there, very easily. The challenge with the top 10 rows of data is the 10 rows of data hardly tell me anything about what is happening in 6 million other rows that exist. The top 10 rows of any data set rarely changes. It's a common part of life.

When I said I really want to know when I make a lot of money; so I can learn from it and take action. The problem is I reverse sorted and it turns out, that's like three people. What am I going to do with these three people? There's nothing I could learn from their behavior that I could use to take action to make more money. I say screw this thing, let me find all the other problems, where I make no money and figure out how to fix it and I sort it the other way. Damn! Screwed again. Again, it's like three people, what am I going to do with it?

This is a very common problem that we face in data. Data's extremities tend to be very sparse. Hence, tends to be very useless. The real magic is in the middle problem, we cannot see 1.6 million rows in this case. All I can see is 10/20, with my glasses on and a large 96-inch monitor, maybe 100 rows. That's it. Yet the magic exists there. The magic to improve peoples' lives and make money, exists there.

So we came up with this hypothesis that the actual values that exist, that are being reported by the solution at the very extremities are not the real values. The behavior of people doesn't exist like that. We said come up with what should be an estimated true value for any particular dimension. If we have enough number of people reporting it, it's probably closer to the site average. If very few people are reporting that data, it's probably much closer to the site average than being the actual value that somebody has reported. Say, somebody said $139 were made by the action of this one person is probably not true in real life. We decided to move away from reporting the actual value and start reporting the estimated true value and the benefit of this is so sexy. Now, I get this little button on top. I press the button, it sorts the data by interesting-ness . . .

It says here are the rows of data. Notice the first and second columns, they're randomly sorted as if using no logic. But the sorting is done based on where we believe now, having analyzed your hundreds and millions of rows of data, the biggest opportunity exists for you to make money in this case. We've gone through tons and tons of data and found for you the highest places to make money and the worst things you have ever created in your life, that you should kill. It would be, very hard to find this data any other way. You can do this in any scenario. Here, we're trying to find out what other BFFs [Best Friends Forever], when it comes to collecting data on the internet and it's very, very easy for us to figure out where we should do advertising, promotions, where we should do different things because the data is now sorted by interestingness.

I love the way this solves the problem of identifying the unknown unknowns. Things you don't even know exist in your data set. In this case, massive opportunities for you to improve life for other people who deal with you; that in turn creates data democracy.

The second solution is even more interesting, for me, personally. Today, when people log into these kinds of tools, i.e., Google Analytics, a massive awesome tool, they run into these problems of data "puking." Every single day you have to figure out what are the things that I need to deal with in order to create actions that will drive better things in our life. What happens is that we naturally gravitate towards this column and probably gravitating towards this column. The way we solve this problem of trying to get people to identify the unknown unknowns, is to say why don't we create an algorithm that is really, really smart, rather than you waking up in the morning saying, the brilliant genius incarnation of the most brilliant genius data scientist that ever lived on earth, why doesn't the system be smart enough to say, let us give you better starting points for your data. Let us apply intelligence.

We've created this algorithm that uses control limits, that has a nice sophisticated forecasting algorithm built in, it does sensitivity analysis of your data and when you wake up in the morning, log into the tool, it actually tells you the known unknowns without you having to do anything. So when you log into Google Analytics, you don't get this data puke. What's more interesting is we said we found interesting things in your data that you don't even know exist. You can highlight them. It's very cool. It says something interesting happened in Germany for this particular piece of data, this particular campaign, this particular page, this particular XYZ. They're really cool things. You can say I don't have a lot of time, only show me data that is six standard deviations away from the mean. Show me things that are super fantastically big, or I have nothing better to do, I've just abandoned my mother, I have all the time in the world, show me even the tiny little things so that I can just spend all day long, wallowing in data. You get to make the choice.

The other thing is, for everything that gets highlighted to tell you what the significance of that result is, either it's really, really important that you pay attention or it's not really important that you pay attention this. And we show you the predictive ranges we've found for these data. We'll tell you that we were anticipating our predictive powers . . . we expected this to be in this particular range, but the real results we received were this and that is *why* you need to pay attention to this thing that happens. It's absolutely amazing because people said this is great, but you're still not telling me what to do. Okay, fine, fine. Not a problem.

Now what we do is actually go into the data and find for you things that are highly correlated that explain this odd behavior that our algorithm has found. So not only do we tell you what the unknown unknowns are, we tell you those unknown unknowns happen because. . . . All you do my sweetheart is have a little lollipop, take some action now. Brilliant, brilliant! We go away from just having people use a tool with billions and billions of tips in it to do data puking, to actually proactively delivering unknown unknowns to them so they could take that action and create a data democracy.

By the way, if you happen to be BFF with Donald Rumsfeld and he loves known unknowns, not a problem, right? We've got a solution built in where you can apply your own brilliance and say just tell me when this happens in the data. You can create all these things, we will highlight for you things that you know will happen, but you don't know when they will happen. We will tell you when they happen and not only puke it at you, we'll tell you what you did to cause that to be an out. Freakin' insane.

I may not be interested in having lots of Big Data. I'm not really interested in having massive heads explode because of the size of the data we have. But I'm really, really interested in what I hypothesize you should be interested in. Trying to figure out how to use that, the intelligence we possess to make life better for the people who are in our companies who deal with the data, who work at our clients and people at the other end who use our products and services. I think if you create a data democracy that is sans data puking, is driven by this quest to find things in the data that other people would never know exist, I really believe that we can empower that kind of action every day that would otherwise be impossible.

Thank you very much.

RECOMMENDED RESOURCES

Books

Bill Franks. *Taming the Big Data Tidal Wave: Finding Opportunities in Huge Data Streams with Advanced Analytics*. Hoboken, NJ: John Wiley & Sons, 2012.
O'Reilly Radar Team. *O'Reilly Media, Big Data Now: Current Perspectives from O'Reilly Radar*. Sebastopol, CA: O'Reilly Media, 2011.
O'Reilly Radar Team. *Ethics of Big Data*. Sebastopol, CA: O'Reilly Media, 2012.
Edd Dumbill. *Big Data*. Mary Ann Liebert, Inc., 2013.

Blogs and Websites

Big Data

- David Smith blog, http://blog.revolutionanalytics.com
- BigDataUniversity, www.bigdatauniversity.com
- IBM Smarter Computing Blog, www.smartercomputingblog.com/category/big-data
- Silicon Angle TV, http://siliconangle.tv/channels/Hadoop
- Top Influencers Big Data, Analytics, Data Mining, www.kdnuggets.com/2012/02/top-influencers-big-data-analytics-data-mining.html

Visualization

- Data Stories, http://datastori.es
- Visual Insights, http://visualinsights.wordpress.com
- Science and Art Big Data Visualization, http://visualinsights.wordpress.com
- Information is Beautiful, www.informationisbeautiful.net
- Jer Thorp, http://blog.blprnt.com
- Flowing Data, http://flowingdata.com/category/visualization/artistic-visualization
- Hint.FM, http://hint.fm
- Data Visualization Tools, http://selection.datavisualization.ch
- Periodic Table of Visualization Methods, www.visual-literacy.org/periodic_table/periodic_table.html

Analysts

- GigaOm, http://gigaom.com
- Forrester Big Data Blog, http://blogs.forrester.com/category/big_data
- Gartner – Doug Laney, http://blogs.gartner.com/doug-laney
- Gartner, Donald Feinberg, http://blogs.gartner.com/donald-feinberg
- O'Reilly, http://oreilly.com
- McKinsey, www.mckinseyquarterly.com/home.aspx

LinkedIn Groups

- Big Data / Analytics / Strategy / FP&A / S&OP / Strategic, www
  .linkedin.com/groups/Big-Data-Analytics-Strategy-FP-1814785?
  home=&gid=1814785&trk=anet_ug_hm
- Big Data, Low Latency, www.linkedin.com/groups/Big-Data-
  Low-Latency-3638279?home=&gid=3638279&trk=anet_ug_hm
- Big Data and Analytics, www.linkedin.com/
  groups?gid=4332669&trk=group-name
- BIG DATA, NoSQL and Cloud Computing Discussion, and JOB
  posting, www.linkedin.com/groups/BIG-DATA-NoSQL-Cloud-
  Computing-3735067?home=&gid=3735067&trk=anet_ug_hm
- Distributed Computing and Applications Professional: Hadoop,
  MapReduce, NoSQL, MongoDB, VLDB, Big Data, www.linkedin
  .com/groups/Distributed-Computing-Applications-Professional-
  Hadoop-2390941/about?report%2Esuccess=b_Iidb5rvC6Fg
  TmwXHFOjqQnqZw7JVoiiNShwRjXZZLuk4GrxWNHM
  UjnWSnBgEvyroPY7nRnZK5fsAGTrMI2RB59LvjMy83T7DCY_
  Pf5QPTB2F8wUW3Jx7bXZh5Dy8owrBNHh_O3WUy6uyO7
  DWzHxnsnqviB2FpTxLSHhc8Occ76wk9sx_gUYwopv-i6Ej87_71Jr
  h6nZK58k2w7MoqJr7sXKZTD24pjtqOc9rY
- HPC and Big Data, www.linkedin.com/groups?gid=110924&mostPo
  pular=&trk=tyah

Conferences and Tradeshows

- GigaOm Structure, GigaOm Structure Data, http://event.gigaom.com
- O'Reilly Strata Conferences + Hadoop World, http://strataconf.com
- Predictive Analytics World, www.predictiveanalyticsworld.com
- Hadoop Summit, http://hadoopsummit.org

ABOUT THE AUTHORS

Michael Minelli is a sales and marketing expert with over 16 years of experience in the business analytics solutions space. Currently, he is Vice President of Sales and Global Alliances, Information Services for MasterCard Advisors, where he is responsible for leading sales and strategic alliances that monetize MasterCard's data assets. MasterCard data assets encompass 1.8 billion cards, representing 34 million merchants in 210 countries and territories. Prior to MasterCard Advisors, Minelli led Revolution Analytics' sales team. He was responsible for both new business development and strategic alliances for the firm's software and services offerings supporting the Open Source R project.

Prior to joining Revolution Analytics, Minelli built his foundation and expertise in analytic solution sales and marketing as he served as a Sales Director and Global Account Manager at SAS. During his 11 years in multiple roles at SAS, he built an extremely successful track record selling large-scale analytic projects associated with customer intelligence, risk management, supply chain, and finance.

Prior to joining SAS, he was a sales executive at MMS, a start-up ERP and business intelligence firm (MMS was acquired in 1999 by AMOS).

Big Data, Big Analytics is Michael Minelli's second book. He is also the coauthor of *Partnering with the CIO: The Future of IT Sales Seen Through the Eyes of Key Decision Makers* (John Wiley & Sons, 2007).

Michael holds a BA in Marketing from Pace University.

Michele Chambers holds a BS in Computer Engineering from Nova Southeastern University and an MBA from Duke University. She is an entrepreneurial executive with 25 years of technology experience. Ms. Chambers was formerly the General Manager and Vice President of Big Data analytics at IBM. Her team was responsible for working with customers to fully exploit the IBM Big Data platform including the IBM Netezza appliance via scalable, high performance advanced analytics on IBM Netezza's parallel computing platform. Ms. Chambers was responsible for guiding the vision, strategy, sales, and go-to-market strategy for IBM Netezza Analytics. Her passion is helping companies identify new areas to apply analytics, especially optimization, that drive high business value and create sustainable differentiation in the market.

Ms. Chambers has a strong focus on results and growth. She has successfully launched several lines of businesses, including the Advanced Analytic Solutions at Netezza, which drove $80 million in revenue in just six months.

Additionally, she successfully built a packaged SAP solutions business resulting in over $10 million revenue in the first year and an early supply chain execution software business.

In her spare time, Ms. Chambers, who is a single mother, loves to show her precocious tween the world and challenge him to make the world a better place by applying his mathematical talents to solve real-world problems.

Ambiga Dhiraj is the Head of Client Delivery for Mu Sigma. Mu Sigma is a leading provider of decision sciences and analytics solutions, helping companies institutionalize data-driven decision making. During her career at Mu Sigma, Ambiga has led Mu Sigma's delivery teams to solve high impact business problems in the areas of Marketing, Supply Chain and Risk Analytics for market-leading companies across multiple verticals. With experience in computer engineering, research, and consulting, she has enabled Mu Sigma to integrate math, business, and technology in a unique manner to develop innovative solutions in the area of decision sciences.

INDEX